RING OF FIRE

THE GUTS AND GLORY OF THE PROFESSIONAL BULL RIDERS TOUR

KENDRA SANTOS

WITH PHOTOGRAPHY BY ANDY WATSON, GARY JENSEN, AND OTHERS

TRIUMPH
BOOKS

CHICAGO

This book is available in quantity at special discounts for your group or organization. For further information, contact:

Triumph Books

601 South LaSalle Street

Suite 500

Chicago, Illinois 60605

(312) 939-3330

Fax (312) 663-3557

Printed in the United States.

ISBN 1-57243-412-0

Book design by Kai's Kreations, Inc.

Photo Credits:
Andy Watson: pages i, vi, 2-9, 11 (right), 12-14, 15 (bottom left), 17 (top right), 18 (left); 20-22, 23 (bottom left and right), 24 (top right and bottom), 25, 26-28, 29 (top left and right), 30 (left), 31 (top left, right), 34, 37-41, 44, 46-48, 50-53, 55 (bottom), 57-58, 62-63, 68-71, 73 (top), 74 (bottom), 77, 78 (top left), 80-81 (center top), 82, 83 (bottom), 88-91, 98-99, 103 (top), 104, 106-108, 109 (top), 110-115, 116 (bottom left), 116-117 (bottom center), 117 (top right), 118-123, 124-125, 126-134, 136, 137 (bottom), 139 (bottom), 147, 148 (top, bottom right), 149, 150-151 (bottom left), 152-153 (left)
Gary Jensen: pages 10 (left), 15 (top left and right), 16, 17 (top and bottom left, bottom right), 29 (bottom), 30 (top right), 36, 42 (left), 43, 45, 46 (top left), 54, 56 (left), 60-61, 64-67, 68 (left), 71 (bottom right), 72 (left), 76, 80 (left), 81 (bottom, top right), 84 (bottom), 92-97, 100-102, 109 (middle left), 117 (bottom right), 124 (top left), 135, 138 (bottom left), 140-141, 148 (bottom left), 150 (top left), 154
Shari Van Alsburg: pages 10-11 (center top and bottom), 19 (right), 23 (top), 24 (top left), 26 (top left), 30 (bottom right), 42 (right), 55 (top right), 56 (bottom right), 59 (bottom right), 72 (top right), 73 (bottom left and right), 109 (bottom right), 116 (top), 137 (top right), 151 (top and bottom right), 153 (top left, bottom right)
Kendra Santos: pages 15 (bottom right), 18-19 (center), 26 (bottom left), 31 (bottom left), 32-33, 56 (top right), 59 (top and bottom left, top right), 74 (top), 75 (bottom), 83 (top right), 103 (bottom), 138 (top left and right), 139 (top left and right)
Professional Bull Riders, Inc.: pages 86 (bottom), 87
Terry Williams: pages 84 (top), 85, 86 (top)
FanCorp, Ink: pages 2 (bottom left), 75 (top), 142-144
Destination Films: pages 145-146
Harry Tompkins: page 79 (bottom left and right)
Jim Shoulders: page 78 (bottom left, top and bottom right)
Larry Mahan: page 79 (top)

TABLE OF CONTENTS

FOREWORD

By James Redford, screenwriter of *Ring of Fire*

For me, childhood was a wellspring of contradictions. During the school year I navigated the streets of Manhattan, which certainly had their share of danger and excitement. Yet it was my childhood summers in Utah that ultimately offered the highest and most rewarding challenges: work on our family ranch, our somewhat daunting, rather green quarter horses, hiking, and camping trips with only bags of raisins, flour, and fishing line to provide food. These were the challenges I preferred, and it is no accident that I have chosen to live my life in the West where, I would argue, these themes run swift and deep within Western culture in general and rodeo culture in particular.

The equation of rodeo is man and beast. For eight dizzying, terrifying, and sometimes deadly seconds the bull rider uses every inch of his mental, physical, and spiritual capacities— not only to ride the bull, but to do it with style and grace.

For the Spanish matador, contact with the bull is reserved for the final coup de grace, a touch wedded to a fatal plunge of steel—a far cry from the bull rider who, in a sense, strives to briefly become a part of the bull. Indeed, in many ways bull riding asks far more of both the bull and the rider than does traditional bullfighting. It asks more from the bull because there is no greater outrage in his mind than being ridden. It asks more from the man because he must not only face the bull but also ride it, armed with little more than his own experience, skill, and courage.

Much has been made of the bull rider's courage. Is it the perfect embodiment of a timeless virtue? Or is it a brazen, macho stupidity? The truth is, it would be a grave mistake to solely embrace either view. Bull riders and their motivations are as varied and independent as the bulls they ride. In the screenplay for Xavier Koller's upcoming movie *Ring of Fire*, Ely Braxton, champion bull rider, is driven in the end by identity. But each and every man who climbs on the back of a bull has his own drive, his own dream. Ultimately, that is what we are watching when the gate swings open: dreams. We sit on the edge of our seats, rooting for the rider, rooting for his dream. And by doing so—whether we are conscious of it or not—we are also rooting for our own.

INTRODUCTION

By Tuff Hedeman, President of the PBR

People always ask me if the PBR's success surprises me. I tell them no. If a few of us cowboys hadn't truly believed that bull riding in its highest form could make it as a stand-alone sport, we never would have taken this chance in the first place.

What does surprise me is how far we've come so fast. When we were riding for $250,000 on our first PBR Tour in 1994, we thought there'd never be another poor day. That kind of money was unheard of back then. And now the 2000 PBR Tour is worth $6.2 million. If you'd told me five years ago that that'd happen, I'd have laughed at you. I believed in this product, but that figure wouldn't have come to me in my wildest dreams. It's beyond amazing, and we have our sponsors, fans, and TNN telecasts to thank for it.

Whether you buy a ticket to be there in person or pull up a chair at home, every PBR event is very exciting to watch. It's a 150-pound cowboy against a 2,000-pound bull, and people want to see the unbelievable rides and the nasty wrecks.

I'm very proud of the fact that success on the PBR Tour is based purely on performance. It's not who you know or what you know—it's what you can get done in the arena that counts. The best guy always wins in the PBR, because there's no way to politic a bull or talk your way into this winner's circle.

Stars drive every major league sport, and bull riding is no different. That goes for the bull riders and the bulls, and the PBR offers fans the best of both. I don't care what business you're in, quality will always sell. When you go to one of our events, you're guaranteed to see the best cowboys on the best bulls. When we were forming this organization, we tried to ask ourselves what the fans want to see. Sitting through a performance of mediocre cowboys on mediocre stock is like going to a Wild West circus. No successful professional sport lets just anyone off the street play. Throwing every level of talent into one pot just dilutes the product. We set PBR up so that riders not only have to earn the right to ride on the Tour but also must maintain that elite performance level on a continual basis. If they don't, they're out. That's fair, and it ensures fans only the best of the best on every front. On any given day, any one of the top forty-five PBR bull riders can win it all. That's been proven time and time again. We have far and away the deepest talent pool in the sport. That's a fact, too. Every bull is a chance at the chips at a PBR event, so it's never a drawing contest around here. It's not about who travels the hardest or who gets lucky and draws the best bull. It's about who rides the best, pure and simple.

Bull riding is about as true a form of sport as I can think of. It's so simple. The meanest, rankest, most athletic, and hard-to-ride bulls from all over the map do everything but pull a gun to get guys on the ground. Both bull and bull rider give it all they've got, but one wins and one doesn't. That's about as straightforward as it gets, and it's great to watch.

The PBR breaks records in every area of operations year after year. Everything about this sport gets bigger and better by the day, from the payoffs to the crowds. But there's a price to be paid in this sport at this level. The injury factor is sky high. The complexion of bull riding has drastically changed for the better in the last few years in every area but injuries. Bull riding has never been more difficult, dangerous, or intense than it is today. The competition has risen to such a high level that you have to try your heart out every single time or you're toast. Unfortunately, that level of intensity doesn't lend itself to long careers for cowboys. There are no days off in the PBR, and it's the guys who are able to handle the bull nobody wants—the bull that there's no telling what he's going to do, that's trying to knock your teeth out or stick a horn in you—who end up wearing the gold buckle. Lots of guys have the talent and ability to be the world champion, but a lot of them don't have the physical and mental toughness it takes to come out on top. At this level of the game, nobody just goes through the motions and wakes up a world champion. You have to want it more than anything else in the world and put your heart and soul into it every day or you don't stand a chance, because the guy who wants it the most will win it.

The PBR has clearly emerged as this sport's major league. We have every person who's ever bought a ticket or tuned us in on TNN to thank for that. I hope everyone is enjoying this ride as much as all of us bull riders are.

TUFF HEDEMAN

PBR cowboys have an unrivaled camaraderie that comes from knowing that their bull-riding brothers risk injury and even death every time they get on a bull. It gets intense in these trenches, so the troops stick together.

The PBR gold buckle is the most coveted cowboy prize there is. He who holds this treasure in his hand rode better throughout the course of an entire year than any other bull rider on the planet. A complete set of bragging rights comes with this buckle, though that right is seldom, if ever, exercised.

CHAPTER 1
WELCOME TO THE PBR

The roadmap of scars on his chin tells you where he's been, and by the look of all those detours it hasn't been an easy trip. But he wouldn't trade the triumphs and tragedies he's met along the way for anything money can buy.

And yes, those two front teeth are fake. They fill in for the pair punched out by a bull's horn before he was old enough to shave. He takes them out when he rides so he won't choke on them, and it's not a pretty sight. But fear not. If all goes according to plan tonight, he'll stick the shiny new ones in there before the cameras fire up for his TV interview.

There's not a whiff of pampered-athlete syndrome within a thousand miles of here. No coaches, no contracts, and definitely no desire to ride the bench. This is PBR country, and wusses need not apply. Talent talks, hot air walks, and excuses get you sent home from the party.

Officially, PBR stands for Professional Bull Riders. It unofficially translates into guts, gore, grit, and, when they dig down deep and try those guts out, glory. When you look at the death-defying cowboy daredevils who take their best shot at a one-ton, snot-snorting, fire-breathing beast that'd just as soon shish kebab them with a horn as let them make the eight-second whistle, it's easy to see why fans don't sit on their hands at a PBR show. Fact is, seats are basically optional on the PBR Tour, and fans spend the better part of this show on their feet, just beyond the edge of their seats.

The top forty-five bull riders in the world earn their way onto the coveted PBR Bud Light Cup Tour, the major league of the sport, and do battle with the toughest, rankest, hardest-to-ride bulls on the planet when they get there.

PBR President Tuff Hedeman is the ultimate bull riding icon. When he welcomes fans to each Bud Light Cup event, the response is as explosive as the fireworks that follow.

The Copenhagen Bull Riders Tough Company Tour serves as the PBR's "farm league" and gives the most talented up-and-comers an equal opportunity to strut their stuff based strictly on each day's performance. After every five Bud Light Cup events, the bottom five cowboys on the Bud Light Cup Tour are replaced by the top five on the Copenhagen Bull Riders Tough Company Tour. In other words, it doesn't matter who you are or what your resume looks like—it's put up or shut up today or step down tomorrow.

The PBR Bud Light Cup Tour showcases the best of the best among both bull riders and bulls. Period. That's fair, and it's FANtastic when it comes to drawing a loyal following. PBR fans pack coliseums from Boston to Bakersfield to follow the thrills, spills, and chills of the PBR Tour. They never leave the arena wondering why sportswriters repeatedly vote bull riding the world's most dangerous sport. Like they've said on TNN's PBR telecasts, which reach another 80 million-plus homes and have everything to do with PBR's skyrocketing popularity, "If PBR doesn't excite you, you better check your pulse."

Corporate America has enthusiastically fanned the flames of the PBR phenomenon. Companies and organizations like Bud Light, Jack Daniel's, the city of Las Vegas, and Wrangler all jumped in with both boots when they spotted the NASCAR-sized potential in the PBR.

It's hard to believe that this astronomical growth started just a few short years ago in a modest hotel room filled with a handful of bull riders who shared a common dream. In 1992, a twenty-head herd of the world's best bull riders got together in that little room and plunked down $1,000 apiece in seed money. They took a chance

on their belief that bull riding, which is rodeo's most popular event, could make it as a stand-alone, professional sport. With four-time World Champion Bull Rider Tuff Hedeman and fellow cowboy legend Cody Lambert at the helm as president and vice president, the cowboy-owned and -operated PBR was born that night.

And my how it's grown!

When PBR contestants rode for $250,000 of prize money on the inaugural 1994 PBR Tour, they thought they had the world by the tail. They were floored when 10 million viewers tuned them in on TNN that year. Of course the basic premise of the original cowboy sport still applies. If you don't ride—and win—you don't get paid. But in 2000, the best bull riders in the business are riding for a record-smashing $6.2 million on the PBR Tour, which includes twenty-eight regular-season Bud Light Cup stops and is capped off by the $1.5 million PBR Bud Light Cup World Championships in Las Vegas.

PBR just might be the fastest growing extreme sport; the only old-fashioned twist is the cowboys' never-say-die-'til-you're-dead attitude. Every show opens with a cutting-edge video and pyrotechnic/laser light show extravaganza. Rock music rolls throughout every action-packed performance and the curtain closes with an in-arena interview with the champ, right down in the dirt. Then, while the dust settles, all forty-five

cowboys return to the arena for an autograph encore, which includes posing for snapshots with fans and autographing everything from the pockets of Wrangler jeans to belly buttons. There's not a prima donna in the bunch; they all know that without the fans there is no sport. These guys don't return to the locker room to pack up their chaps and spurs until the last fan leaves with a smile on his or her face.

The young guns of the PBR have created a bond with those who share their love for the sport. There's a mutual respect and appreciation going on here, and you can feel that electricity in every building they enter.

In another departure from traditional rodeo, where the world champions are determined based on how much money contestants win, the PBR has set up their world championship points system to ensure that it's the cowboy who delivers the most consistently spectacular performance over the course of the year who comes out king. The fundamentals of judging bull riding work like this: Each of two arena judges (four at the Finals) mark each ride using a scale of 1–25 points for how hard the bull bucks and another 1–25 points for how handily the cowboy covers him. The combined scores equal a possible 100 points. A third judge is stationed on the back of the chutes and holds the official stopwatch. Besides determining whether or not each rider makes the required eight-second whistle, he also watches for fouls and writes down his

The PBR is a pyromaniac's prayer answered. But like PBR Bud Light Cup Series Manager Tommy Joe Lucia says, "The live event has to be bigger and better than what one can see in his living room. With that in mind, we've attempted to develop a production that matches the intensity of the sport. That's why the first fifteen minutes of the show is pure energy."

lets his riding do his talking for him. "I can't even say how good winning the PBR world championship made me feel," said the Lordsburg, New Mexico, cowboy. "It was everything I wanted in life. But if I'd shown the feelings I had inside, I would have looked like a total idiot."

Then there was Michael "G-Man" Gaffney's championship year in 1997. Gaffney overcame what appeared to be an insurmountable lead built by Moraes over the regular season with a gutsy, late-season charge. Moraes sat helplessly on the sidelines at that year's Finals with a broken leg but, true to the PBR's sporting, "may the best man win" philosophy, he cheered his friend to victory and shook Gaffney's hand when he stepped up on stage.

"You can't fake what we do," said Gaffney, who calls Corrales, New Mexico, home. "Your odds of dribbling down the court with a basketball and scoring a shot are pretty good. But in the PBR, the odds are stacked way against you. It's exciting, and it's never the same thing twice because there's an animal involved and there's no staging what we do. It's man against beast, pure and simple, and you can expect the unexpected."

PBR's international flavor flared up again in 1998, when Australian champion Troy Dunn added the PBR world championship to his lengthy list of bull-riding achievements. The gritty Dunn took the title based on his domination in the regular season. A dislocated hip suffered in the opening round at that year's Finals forced him to the sidelines for the remainder of the year. But Dunn was not to be denied.

"This is the one," said Dunn, who hails from the town of Mackay in Queensland, Australia. "It's the championship everyone wants. If you

own score, which is used to break ties going into the short round and determine which bull each of the deadlocked cowboys will ride.

"Consistency is probably the most important trait of a good judge," said PBR Vice President Cody Lambert, who often serves as the third judge on the back of the chute. "A good judge should be able to mark a ride the same whether it's cold and rainy outside and there's no one in the stands, or you're indoors with fifteen thousand people screaming and standing. A judge has to make some unpopular decisions at times, like when someone makes a flawless ride on a bull that's never been ridden before, but the bull stumbles and the rider slaps him [with his free hand]. He can't mark that ride. He also has to be strong enough to give a guy a low score when he rides a bull that's seldom if ever ridden, if that bull didn't have his day that day."

The PBR has crowned six world champions to date. In 1994, Brazilian bombshell Adriano Moraes became the first to wear the ultimate bull-riding crown. "PBR is the greatest thing,"

Moraes said with his strong Brazilian accent. "It's the best of everything, from the bulls and riders to the money, the format, and the friendships. We're like a big family. I love the PBR."

In 1995 Tuff Hedeman took the PBR gold and added it to his collection of world championship buckles from the Professional Rodeo Cowboys Association, dated 1986, 1989, and 1991. "Nothing has ever thrilled or excited me more than riding bulls," said Hedeman, who hangs his hat in Morgan Mill, Texas. "I've always said the whistle cures all ills. We had a lot of incentive to grow this sport, because bull riders have shorter careers than other cowboys. It's only natural, because we take a lot more risks every time we get on than the guys in the other events do. You have to get it while you can. In this sport, one day you're the king, the next you're just another guy eating a cheeseburger."

Hot on Hedeman's heels with the 1996 PBR world title was Owen Washburn. No doubt the most soft-spoken PBR champ yet, Washburn

don't want this one, you don't want to ride bulls."

Cody Hart sent the record books packing in 1999. After winning an unprecedented six Bud Light Cup events during the regular season, he had his first world championship wrapped up before the Finals even rolled around. "PBR isn't about drawing the best bull or traveling the hardest, and there are no politics," said Hart of Walnut Bend, Texas. "PBR makes it simple. We all get on great bulls and the best guy wins. There's more money and less travel [than in traditional rodeo], and it's the best bull riders in the world against the best bulls.

You don't win the PBR title because you entered right or drew good, you win it because you rode the best. That's why the PBR title is now the most respected title there is—if you come out on top, there's a reason."

The current PBR board of directors includes President Hedeman, Vice President Lambert, Jerome Davis, Ty Murray, Michael Gaffney, Troy Dunn, and Aaron Semas.

"Bull riding's fun to watch because it's thrilling and totally unpredictable," said Murray, a founding PBR shareholder. "The rules are simple, too—you either make the

whistle without getting drilled or you don't. A girl who never watched a hockey game and doesn't know what's going on is lost. But she can go to a bull-riding event and get right into the game.

"There's no secret to PBR's success. All we've done is use common sense. The main thing is we've never lost sight of our mission statement, which says we're going to have the very best guys and the very best bulls at every event. It's been pretty easy to do, because if you're a professional, world-class bull rider who's qualified to ride on this Tour and you don't show up, you're stupid."

The cowboys aren't the only ones with adrenaline bouncing through their bodies at PBR events. Rowdy opening ceremonies that include video, light, laser, and pyrotechnic extravaganzas set the raucous stage for the thrills, chills, and spills that follow.

PBR cowboy K. J. Pletcher, who normally would rather be caught naked in the middle of Main Street than wear a "drugstore cowboy" hat like this one, couldn't turn down a friendly dare. He was challenged to wear this "Ned Gump" lid at the Jerome Davis Challenge in Charlotte, North Carolina, and Davis got a big hoot out of it.

The locker room is a zoo zone. Before every performance, cowboys check their equipment and show their support for PBR sponsor partners by plastering their protective vests with logos.

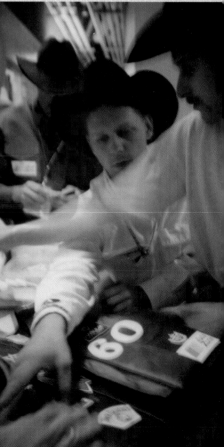

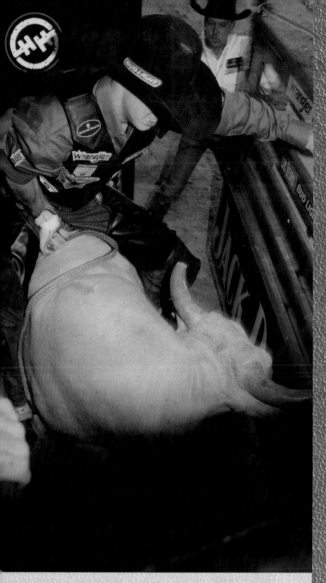

Chin tucked, wrap taken, and free arm at the ready, Kansas cowboy Jesse Schellhamer nods for his draw at the 1999 PBR Bud Light Cup World Championships. The first jump out of the chute feels like a cannon blast.

Brock Mortensen pays tribute to his fallen friend Glen Keeley, who was killed March 24, 2000, by the hooves of a bull. In Keeley's memory, Mortensen proudly wears Keeley's name, his vest number (68), and a yellow ribbon that promises never to forget.

1997 Ty Murray Invitational, back when Terry Williams owned the bull. Hedeman gunned down every great bull going in his career, yet also deeply respected them for their athletic excellence.

Tuff Hedeman won four world championships, including the 1995 PBR world title, in his storied career. He came back from injuries most mortals might not have survived, but a second broken neck in 1998 drew the line for him and ended his bull riding career.

It's been said that Tuff Hedeman "rode ugly." Fact is, he did whatever it took to get the job done and didn't concern himself much with style points. His never-say-die attitude took him to heights all his own.

PBR Vice President Cody Lambert, who, since hanging up his chaps in 1996, often serves as a judge, checks his score sheets as bullfighter Jimmy Anderson looks on. As a judge it's Lambert's job to make sure the money lands in the right pockets.

Cody Lambert also serves as the PBR Livestock Director. In that capacity he searches coast to coast for the buckingest bulls in the business. The greatest bulls on earth are the only opponents worthy of showcasing the world's best bull riding talent, so Lambert hauls them in from far and wide.

There's never been a better bull rider or a more popular cowboy than Tuff Hedeman. He wowed crowds like no one else and continues to stick around after every performance until the very last fan in the place has left with an autograph and a smile.

PBR President Tuff Hedeman is a workhorse who goes at growing the PBR powerhouse 24/7. The PBR wouldn't exist without him, and it's because of him that it's not only survived but also thrived. Some say he might as well have a cell phone surgically attached to his ear.

Jerome Davis tackles Red Wolf for 92.5 points in the short round at the St. Louis Open. With four rides in the 90s apiece, Davis and Adriano Moraes were the 1997 Copenhagen Bull Riders 90-Point Club co-champions.

Jerome Davis won the 1995 PRCA world bull riding championship, and there's no telling how many more gold buckles he might have got under his belt had his career not been cut short by a paralyzing bull riding wreck in the spring of 1998.

The lights went out when, on March 14, 1998, Jerome Davis smashed heads with Jerry Nelson's bull Knock 'em Out John at Tuff Hedeman's Championship Challenge in Fort Worth. The blow knocked Davis out. Then a drilling into the dirt—head first—caused a fracture/dislocation of the sixth and seventh vertebrae at the base of his neck. Davis was paralyzed from the chest down. These days Davis' gold-buckle spirit gets him through. He can't use his legs, but his heart's bigger than ever. One of the PBR's original founding members, Davis continues to serve on the PBR Board of Directors and hosts the Jerome Davis Challenge in Charlotte, North Carolina, each June.

Just another day at the office for Jerome Davis in his prime. This shot was taken at the Bud Light Cup stop in Boise, Idaho. As a bull rider, Davis had it all—strength, athleticism, and an iron will that never let him down.

Tater Porter, Cody Hart, and Jerome Davis talked shop atop the chutes at the 1997 Jerome Davis Challenge, when Davis was a serious contender for the PBR crown. A year later Davis would enter that same arena in a wheelchair.

Ty Murray stepped up on stage twice to receive his 1999 PBR Finals buckle from announcer Bob Feist, first in front of Finals fans in the Thomas and Mack Center Arena right after the final performance and then again at the awards banquet that night at Caesars Palace.

The thrill of victory was major-league sweet for an understandably elated Ty Murray, shown here just after stepping off his last bull at the 1999 PBR Finals. Moments later the King of the Cowboys was $265,912 richer and had notched yet another record for annual PBR earnings with $395,795.

In a meeting of two bull riding masterminds, 1997 PBR World Champion Michael Gaffney and his successor, 1998 PBR Champ of the World Troy Dunn, shared scouting reports on the bulls they'd drawn one night at the 1999 PBR Finals.

Michael Gaffney made the humblest of champions. "G" gutted it out in the clutch and came through to take the coveted Bud Light Cup.

Michael "G-Man" Gaffney gets the PBR congeniality award. Gracious in both victory and defeat, he's been a popular 'poke with cowboys and crowds alike throughout his career. Here, he pays his respects to his four-footed foe after another money ride.

Michael Gaffney made good on the long shot Hail Mary play at season's end in 1997. Adriano Moraes built what appeared to be an insurmountable lead over the course of the season while Gaffney quietly trailed. Even when Moraes broke his leg that August, Gaffney needed to create major magic to pull it off—which he did.

Michael Gaffney takes to the rafters on his wild ride to the top. Plagued more than his fair share by injuries throughout his career, his talents finally had enough time away from the bright lights of the operating table to truly shine.

Troy Dunn won his second PBR Bud Light Cup World Championships average crown with this then-record 95-point ride on Red Wolf at the 1997 Finals. Dunn is the only cowboy ever to win the PBR Finals twice.

Troy Dunn was an all-around champion in his native Australia before pulling up stakes and adopting Texas as his second home for a few years. He was tops on his home turf but wanted to try his hand against the best in the business in the PBR. It was the only way to find out if he truly was the best in the world.

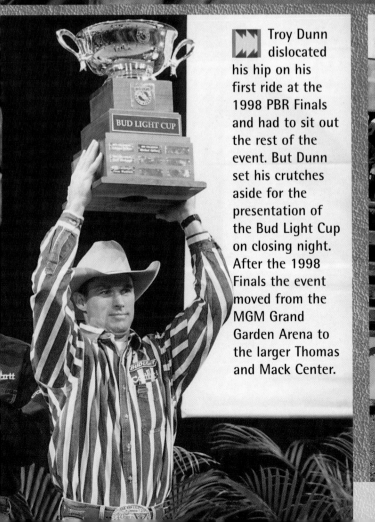

Troy Dunn dislocated his hip on his first ride at the 1998 PBR Finals and had to sit out the rest of the event. But Dunn set his crutches aside for the presentation of the Bud Light Cup on closing night. After the 1998 Finals the event moved from the MGM Grand Garden Arena to the larger Thomas and Mack Center.

After his debilitating Finals wreck in 1998, Troy Dunn trained hard and came back with a vengeance in 1999. Here he is twisting a tall one at the 1999 PBR Finals.

Aaron Semas readies his rope with rosin before a ride. The rosin used by riders gives their gloves some "grab," and helps them avoid popping their hands out of the rope, which still happens anyway at times at this level of the game (right).

Aaron Semas is always a player on the PBR front. On any given day, he'll take the money and run with rides like these (above left and bottom).

Aaron Semas loves life on the edge. He's an extreme sports enthusiast, be it bull riding in the arena or jeep mountain marathons in the high country.

Adriano Moraes and Troy Dunn, shown here visiting from a perch atop the bucking chutes at the 1999 PBR Finals, have a lot in common. They gave up their respective homelands of Brazil and Australia for long stretches of time in their quest to be No. 1—and got there. Moraes spoke only Portuguese when he arrived on American soil, so he got by on hand gestures and cowboy camaraderie for the first year or two. No one said it would be easy, but ask him and he'll tell you—it was worth it.

Brazilian bombshell Adriano Moraes and ultratalented Texan Tuff Hedeman don't share the same accent, but both are passionate about their sport. And both own PBR gold buckles: Moraes' is dated 1994; Hedeman's 1995.

Even the strongest men in the sport are no match for bulls who outweigh them ten times over. Adriano Moraes has taken his share of hookings right along with the rest of the cowboy herd. It's just part of what they call "paying your dues."

Defending PBR World Champion Owen Washburn survived a wicked case of spotted fever at the 1997 Bud Light Cup stop in Billings, Montana. At 6'2", Washburn is one of the tallest bull riders you'll ever see.

The spotlight has never been Owen Washburn's bag. He understands it's part of the package, but it's the riding he really loves. By watching him in public, you get the feeling he'd be happiest at home on the range—on his ranch in New Mexico.

Host Ty Murray presents 2000 Ty Murray Invitational winner Owen Washburn with all the loot that comes with the big bucks at that event. To win the event Washburn had to get by reigning PBR Bucking Bull of the Year Promise Land, who had killed fellow bull rider Glen Keeley the night before. It was a bittersweet victory for Washburn, the 1996 PBR world champion, and one he dedicated to Keeley.

Owen Washburn stepping into the PBR "Ring of Fire" at the 1997 PBR Bud Light Cup World Championships in Las Vegas. An injured Ty Murray, front and center, greeted each contestant as his name was announced.

Cody Hart's no hot dog, but confidence is key in this sport. With it, along with a truckload of talent, you stand a chance. Without it, you're dust.

It's cowboy custom to throw your hat in the air as the cherry on a sundae-perfect ride. Cody Hart liked his effort on this ride and wanted to celebrate, but felt compelled to hoof it out of harm's way first. Every good cowboy knows that the party doesn't start until he's safely out of the arena.

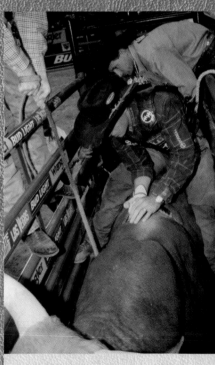

With help from a few friends, Cody Hart prepares to take his wrap at the 1999 PBR Finals. His unbelievable regular season helped Hart wrap up the PBR world championship before the Finals even started. A competitor to the end, he didn't believe it until he held the gold buckle in his hand.

Cody's Cup: Cody Hart tipped the Bud Light Cup at 1999 PBR Finals end. Hart, twenty-two, won a record six regular-season Bud Light Cup events en route to the PBR crown, which is far and away the highlight of his young career.

Cody Hart and Ty Murray were the pride of the PBR in 1999. Besides going at it neck-and-neck in the world championship race all season long, they delivered on demand when the heat was on at the Finals. Hart and Murray finished first and second in the PBR world standings; world runner-up Murray won the Finals.

There was no stopping Cody Hart in 1999, and this is a perfect example of why. Hart's upper body's back when the bull's kicking up in back, and he's in perfect position to move forward with the bull when he comes up in front to take his next jump.

The PBR Board of Directors, along with several big-name sponsor representatives, surround 1999 Champ of the World Cody Hart at the PBR Finals.

A little dust never hurt a guy. Just ask 1998 PBR World Champion Troy Dunn, shown here making a ride in his championship season.

CHAPTER 2
THE FINALS

Baseball has its World Series. Football has its Super Bowl. Bull riding has its PBR Bud Light Cup World Championships. Held each fall since its 1994 debut in the city that's "Open 24 Hours," Las Vegas, the PBR Finals has grown richer and more popular every year. Like the PBR world champions roster, the PBR Bud Light Cup World Championships winners list reads like a "Who's Who" of the sport.

Bull-riding great Ted Nuce topped the inaugural PBR Finals, which was worth a then-impressive $125,000, in 1994. "We're building our own business here," said Nuce, the 1985 Professional Rodeo Cowboys Association world champion bull rider and an original PBR shareholder. "That's more motivating than anything. I want to see this thing reach heights no one ever suspected."

Relative unknown Ronny Kitchens took to the stars and catapulted himself into the driver's seat of the 1996 PBR Rookie of the Year race after winning $130,950 of his $143,298 earnings that year at the PBR Finals.

"This is a feeling most twenty-year-olds will never have," said an elated Kitchens at the close of the 1996 Finals. "To feel this way takes most people a lifetime. It's just unreal for a small-town guy like me to win something like this. You could fit Kemp [his Texas hometown, population seventy-five] inside the [MGM] Grand Garden Arena [home of the PBR Finals until it moved to the Thomas and Mack Center in 1999]."

On both sides of Kitchens in the Finals champion category is Troy Dunn, the only cowboy ever to come out as king of the PBR Finals twice. In 1995 Dunn bagged the $50,000 Finals average champ's check that, added to go-round checks and Bud Light bonus checks, totaled $71,975.

"This is by far the best check I've ever won," Dunn said. "With all the money up, those bulls, and all the pressure, I knew it'd be tough. That last ride felt so good I nearly felt guilty about it. The PBR is the best thing that ever happened to bull riders. If this doesn't excite you, it's time to hang it up."

Dunn doubled down with a second PBR Bud Light Cup World Championships win in 1997, giving Finals fans yet another glimpse at the great gold buckle feats that would follow. "This is even better than the last one because the competition's getting better and better," said Dunn, just after bailing off his last bull.

"Everything about the PBR gets better every year. The bulls do, too, if that's possible."

The "doubled down" part is literal, by the way. In the two years between Dunn's Finals wins, the average prize jumped from $50,000 to $100,000. All told, Dunn returned to his home down under $158,711 richer that year.

On opening day of the 1998 World Championships, the odds of soft-spoken Reed Corder winning the Finals were set at 40-to-1. But this long shot went from underdog to wonderdog overnight, pocketing a record $172,200 in the Finals arena.

"This is the greatest moment of my career," said Melvin, Texas, native Corder, who was nearly as stunned as the oddsmakers themselves. "It easily tops everything else. The money's awesome, but I think the prestige of winning it is the best part of the whole deal. There's no greater feeling in the world than being 90 points. What's really neat is I think the fans love PBR as much as the bull riders do."

Ty Murray, AKA "The King of the Cowboys," has rewritten just about every record there is when it comes to professional rodeo, and many of his accomplishments have been achieved under the Thomas and Mack roof, which is also home to the PRCA's National Finals Rodeo. Some say they ought to take the T & M of the Thomas & Mack Center and rename the place the Ty Murray Center. Considering all the magical moments Murray's pulled out of his hat in that building, it sounds like a reasonable request. The only cowboy ever to win seven PRCA world all-around championships, Murray, who also owns a pair of PRCA world bull-riding championships, has won it all and done it all when it comes to rodeo's roughstock events (which include bareback riding, saddle bronc riding, and bull riding).

He's turned his focus toward the PBR in the last few years, and it shows. In 1999 he notched not only the PBR Finals earnings record with $265,912, but also a PBR annual earnings record of $395,795 to boot. "The 1999 PBR Finals was the best bull-riding competition that's ever been held," said Murray, an Arizona native who now calls the Cowboy Capital of the World—Stephenville, Texas—home. "They rode every great bull there is that week."

Over the course of the four-day, five-round, $1.5 million Finals, Murray won or placed on all five bulls and, with 458 points on

five rides, pulled off a 13.5-point margin of victory over the stellar PBR pack. "It was just a four-day blast," Murray said. "The Finals is what I've competed for since I was a little kid. It's what I've competed for from the junior rodeo and Little Britches level through the high school, college, and National Finals Rodeo level. No NFL player doesn't want to go to the Super Bowl, and no professional bull rider doesn't want to go to the PBR Finals."

"Ty once again proved to everyone what a few of us have known for a long time,"

added PBR Vice President Cody Lambert. Lambert took Murray under his rodeo wing back in 1988, when Murray was a rodeo rookie, and traveled with him until Lambert retired at the end of the 1996 PBR season. "Besides being the greatest all-around cowboy ever, he's the man to beat in bull riding, too. He already has nine gold buckles, has won the NFR in two different events, and now has won more money bull riding than anyone has ever won in one year. At the Finals, he dominated. If there's anyone out there who still questions whether Ty can ride the rank ones, there's your answer."

Murray and Cajun sensation Chris Shivers were neck-and-neck in the world championship race heading into the 2000 PBR Bud Light Cup World Championships.

"I hope the money records get broken every year," Murray said. "The money in the PBR is great and it just keeps getting better. The money's going into the right pockets, too. This sport's going in the right direction as far as the cowboys are concerned and the sponsors and fans are getting a lot more bang for their buck, too."

Troy Dunn looks like a scale as he balances baby son Lathen Grady in one hand and his second PBR Finals buckle in the other at the 1997 Finals. Dunn was also PBR's Touring Pro Division champion in 1997. The TPD, now the Copenhagen Bull Riders Tough Company Tour, is PBR's farm league, although there really isn't a true minor league in the PBR.

Ronny Kitchens came from nowhere—literally, as he hails from Kemp, Texas, population seventy-five—to pull off a Cinderella story of victory at the 1996 PBR Finals. Down and out more times than not with injuries in recent years, one of Kitchens' true trademarks is the way he sticks his tongue way out when he rides.

True to form, Troy Dunn tends not to give up and let go until the back of his head hits the ground. That grit and scrappiness have taken him to the top of the sport.

www. pbrnow.com   THE OFFICI

CRIPPLE CREEK

BUD LIGHT

PBR
PROFESSIONAL BULL RIDERS

Reed Corder is as quiet as they come. But he let his riding do his talking for him at the 1998 PBR Finals, and it was borderline obnoxious. Corder headed home to Melvin, Texas—population 180—with a then-record $172,200 after placing in the first four rounds with 90-plus points on every ride.

The King of the Cowboys was escorted into the arena by a couple of Caesar's finest as he prepared to do battle at the 1999 PBR Bud Light Cup World Championships. Caesars Palace is PBR's home away from home in Las Vegas.

Reed Corder showing off the spoils of victory—his 1998 Bud Light Cup World Championships belt buckle.

Reed Corder was a forty-to-one long shot on opening night of the 1998 PBR Bud Light Cup World Championships. Closing night was a whole different story, however, and his dad, Buddy, who'd plunked down a $200 bet on his boy, was $8,000 richer.

Unless his hand's in a bull rope, Ty Murray never takes life too seriously. He doesn't worry about things he can't control and he loves to laugh every chance he gets.

Cody "Klete" Lambert and Ty "Pud" Murray behind the chutes at the 1996 Jerome Davis Challenge in Charlotte, North Carolina, the last year Lambert rode bulls. Lambert and Murray traveled together from Murray's rookie year as a professional in 1988 until Lambert retired in 1996.

Ted "Teddy Bear" Nuce was winding down his riding career when the PBR really got rolling. Here he is giving James Harper's Judge Ito the third degree at the 1996 Jerome Davis Challenge in Charlotte, North Carolina.

Ty Murray makes a move for the moon at the 1998 PBR Bud Light Cup World Championships. After juggling his rodeo and bull riding schedules for several years, Murray focused his entire 2000 season on the PBR and bull riding. The King of the Cowboys is also the King of the Thomas and Mack Center. Ty Murray, the greatest all-around cowboy of all time, won a record seven PRCA world all-around titles and two PRCA world bull riding championships under the roof of the Thomas and Mack Center before winning the PBR Finals there in 1999. Some say the T and M really stand for Ty Murray instead of Thomas and Mack.

J.W. Hart is considered the Cal Ripken of the PBR. He's the only cowboy never to miss a Bud Light Cup event in his career.

CHAPTER 3
OTHER LEGENDS OF THE PBR

PBR ROOKIES OF THE YEAR

Bull riding is a young man's sport, and dozens of fresh-faced cowboys hit the PBR scene every year in hopes of becoming the next true champion. Since 1995 the PBR has named and honored one such freshman each year as the PBR Rookie of the Year.

Past recipients of the PBR Rookie of the Year award include J.W. Hart in 1995, Ronny Kitchens in 1996, Keith Adams in 1997, Pete Hessman in 1998, and Mike White in 1999.

White earned both the PBR Rookie of the Year honors and the PRCA world bull-riding championship in 1999. He also became the first cowboy ever to take both PBR and PRCA rookie honors (his PRCA honors came in 1997). One of only three cowboys (Ty Murray and Chris Shivers were the other two) to make the whistle on all five bulls at the 1999 PBR Finals, White won $145,164 in the 1999 season. "I'm more interested in the joy and challenge of the ride than the money that comes with the success," said White, who also won the bull-riding average at the 1999 National Finals Rodeo.

White, a Louisiana native who now lives on a ranch in Dekalb, Texas, which he bought with bull-riding earnings in 1999, has a one-track mind that revolves completely around the bovine breed. If he's not riding a bull, he's tending to his herd. "I've always loved being around cows," he said. "I know a lot of guys have other hobbies. I hate a lot of that stuff. I love the ranching life. I'm just an old country boy."

BROTHERLY LOVE

There are four sets of siblings who compete regularly on the PBR Bud Light Cup Tour. Texans Cody and J.W. Hart and Adam and Gilbert Carrillo, Australians Troy and Owen Dunn, and Montanans Judd and Brock Mortensen pull each other's bull ropes and pull for each other in general while shooting at the same big bucks all season long.

"Owen sure helps me," Troy Dunn said of his little brother. "He pumps me up and he knows what to say and when to say it. Owen's always there when I need him. If I'm in a slump, he tells me to wake up. That's better than having someone make excuses

for you. It's also good for me to be around Owen as I get further down the line in my career because he still has the fire. He'll talk about bull riding 'til the cows come home."

The 5'4" identical Carrillo twins are neighbors in Stephenville, Texas, and you can consider it a rare sight if you get a glimpse of one without the other. "Adam and I are like one," said Gilbert, who's five minutes older than Adam. "It's us competing against everybody else. We're partners. If I do good, the bank does good. If he does good, the bank does good. If we both do good, the bank does really good. We share everything. You name it, we share it. We're so close. We lived in a big house when we were kids, but we shared a room because we wanted to. Adam's always in my corner. We always back each other, good or bad. Life's twice as good because of Adam."

J.W. "Hit Man" Hart has earned a reputation as "PBR's Cal Ripken" by being the only bull rider never to miss a PBR Bud Light Cup event since 1995. He and little brother Cody "Wild Man" Hart, the 1999 PBR champ of the world, have set the PBR world on fire since their respective splashdowns. "I think having a brother on the tour with you is a big advantage for sure," J.W. said. "Cody and I build fences together, buy bulls together, and everything else. We have two chances to hay the cows good next week; two shots at the money. I guess there are days when being brothers is a disadvantage, though, like when one wins and the other one has to go home and listen to it. It's a ribbing contest with us. But that's just brotherly love."

RECORD RIDES

The Tampa Open in Tampa Bay, Florida, was the scene of the two rides that share the 96.5-point PBR record. In 1999 Bubba Dunn rode that year's PBR Bucking Bull of the Year, Promise Land, for 96.5 big ones in the final round of competition and took sole possession of the magical milestone.

"He went two [rounds] to the left, and stayed in it [the spin] the full eight seconds," recalled Dunn, who lives about twenty-five miles out of Alexandria, Louisiana. "I was spurring on him a little bit and he was bucking hard. When I hit the ground I was glad to make the whistle. That short-round whistle had been haunting me pretty good."

The first person Dunn saw when he got to his feet was PBR Vice President Cody Lambert, who's never been known to waste a word on anyone or anything he didn't truly believe in. "Cody said, 'That's the best damn bull ride I've ever seen,'" Dunn recalled. "I just thought to myself, 'Wow.'"

Dunn's close friend and traveling partner, Chris Shivers, answered his 96.5-point challenge at the 2000 Tampa Open on the famed Jim Jam. Jim Jam was a bull I've always wanted to get on," said Shivers, the pride of Jonesville, Louisiana. "At first I was a little scared of what he would feel like because I have seen some great guys get bucked off of him who just shouldn't get bucked off."

Only one other man, two-time PRCA World Champion Bull Rider Jim "Razor" Sharp, ever twisted Jim Jam for the full eight seconds. Sharp cranked 94 points out of the four-footed keg of dynamite in round two of the 1999 PBR World Championships.

"I've always liked being 90 or nothing," said Shivers, the 1998 Copenhagen Bull Riders 90-Point Club champion with thirteen 90-pointers that season. "That's how you win first."

THE PBR RING OF HONOR

True legends are rare in any sport. They're the athletes people still talk about decades after they have left the arena. There's a very special place in the heart of the PBR for those who made the sport what it is today, those who shone beyond brilliance both inside the arena and out, and those who have continued to give back to the game long after their riding days were over.

In 1996 the first PBR Ring of Honor presentations were made to Cody Lambert, who retired from a brilliant bull-riding career at the end of that year's PBR Finals but who continues to enter—and win—in the saddle bronc riding event on occasion; Ted Nuce, who qualified for the PRCA's National Finals Rodeo fourteen straight times from 1982 to 1995, a record he shares with the great Wacey Cathey; sixteen-time World Champion Cowboy Jim Shoulders; and fellow ProRodeo Hall of Famer Harry Tompkins.

"The PBR Ring of Honor is about recognizing the guys who've helped make bull riding the sport it's become," said PBR President Tuff Hedeman. "When we were kids, Jim Shoulders and Harry Tompkins were the champs. They gave us something to shoot at. People tend to forget—we don't want to. We need to recognize what and who got us here."

The ring itself is crafted on the same grand scale as Super Bowl rings, with diamonds in a gold setting, and features the PBR logo along with the recipient's name and the year in which he was honored.

Eight-time PRCA World Champion Bull Rider Donnie Gay stepped into the PBR Ring of Honor circle in 1997. Jerome Davis, the 1995 PRCA world champ and a constant contender in the PBR standings until 1998, when he was paralyzed in a bull-riding wreck, was honored in 1998. Also honored that year was Larry "Bull" Mahan, who won six PRCA world all-around championships and two PRCA world bull-riding titles in the 1960s and '70s. The PBR Ring of Honor Class of 1999 included Tuff Hedeman, AKA "The Michael Jordan of Bull Riding"; his late, great best friend, 1987 PRCA World Champion Lane Frost, who died in the arena at the 1989 Cheyenne, Wyoming, Frontier Days Rodeo after taking a horn in the back; and eleven-time NFR bull rider and PBR Production Manager Jerome Robinson.

"The PBR Ring of Honor is a way of honoring the guys we feel achieved greatness in this sport," said a gung ho Tuff Hedeman. "The PBR Ring of Honor is a very elite and prestigious award. There are a lot of great cowboys and bull riders. These guys took time out when they didn't have to give back to the sport. They visited with fans and were very unselfish. That's rare and we want to recognize it."

Although for years Hedeman refused the obvious recognition he himself deserved, the PBR Board of Directors, which serves as the PBR Ring of Honor selection committee, finally overrode Hedeman's presidential powers and had his ring made despite his humble resistance. Hedeman was nearly speechless. So his fellow legends and friends stepped up and spoke for him. "In my mind, Tuff's the greatest bull rider that's ever ridden," Lambert stated. "And he's been a major factor in taking this sport to the level it's at now and the level it'll be at years from now."

Well said.

The PBR Rookie of the Year award goes to the freshman cowboy who wins the most money in his first season on the tour. When Ronny Kitchens won $130,950 at the 1996 PBR Finals, there was no contest. Kitchens, who owed it all to his phenomenal Finals performance, earned $143,298 for the year.

In 1997, Keith Adams became the third straight Texan to take PBR Rookie of the Year honors. Since his rookie year, he's been sidelined extensively with injuries.

BUD LIGHT   LAS VEGAS

JACK DANIEL'S

Wrangler®

Pete Hessman, the 1998 PBR Rookie of the Year, is a true cowboy. When he's not on the back of a bull at a PBR event you can usually find him on a horse, working cattle at home in Dodge City, Kansas.

"Pistol Pete" Hessman high-fives bullfighter Roach Hedeman, Tuff's big brother, at the 1999 PBR Finals. They call Hessman "Pistol Pete" because he likes to fire off a few make-believe rounds after every great ride.

Mike White, a native Cajun who in 2000 made the move to a Dekalb, Texas, ranch bought with bull-riding earnings, accepts his 1999 PBR Rookie of the Year buckle from Cody Lambert at the Finals. White was also the 1999 PRCA world champion bull rider. He's the only cowboy ever to win a PRCA gold buckle in combination with PBR rookie honors the same year. He suffered a broken neck in July 2000 at the Days of '47 PRCA Rodeo in Salt Lake City, but planned to heal up and head back out to the arena ASAP.

▶▶ Mike White racks up points
at the Lane Frost Memorial
PBR Bud Light Cup event in
Richmond, Virginia, as PBR
President Hedeman looks on.
Hedeman was Frost's best friend
before Frost's 1989 arena death.

For years, J.W. and Cody Hart shared a joint Hart brothers bull riding account. They liked to say that when one or the other won, "the cows ate good the next week. When we both won, the banker smiled from ear to ear."

When PBR sponsor Double-H Boots came along in search of appropriate cowboy ambassadors, they found the perfect Double-H pair in Cody and J.W. Hart.

Adam Carrillo puts everything he's got into making sure Gilbert gets out of the chute clean at the 1999 PBR Bud Light Cup World Championships.

Brothers Cody and J.W. Hart shared a sentimental moment at the 1999 PBR Finals when, together, they first laid eyes on Cody's PBR gold buckle. It was hard to say who was happier or prouder at that moment.

Brotherly Love: Cody "Wild Man" Hart and J.W. "Hit Man" Hart share a big old bear hug at the 1999 PBR Finals just after Cody's coronation as the new PBR champ of the world.

The way brothers Carrillo and Hart see it, there's strength in numbers. In other words, their odds of winning are twice as good as anyone else's!

Gilbert Carrillo scrambles
out of no man's land at the
1999 PBR Finals. Somewhere back
behind the chutes, Adam is one
worried twin right about now.

Teeth guard in place, Troy Dunn gets his game face on at the PBR Finals. These days, Dunn is busy promoting Championship Bull Riders, which is his Australian answer to the PBR.

"I always ride better when Troy's there," says Owen Dunn, left. "There's a lot of competition between any two brothers in any sport. Troy beats me most of the time, but I can't let him win every time."

Brock Mortensen after an 82.5-
point ride on Casper Baca's Aztec
in round two of the 1998 PBR Finals.

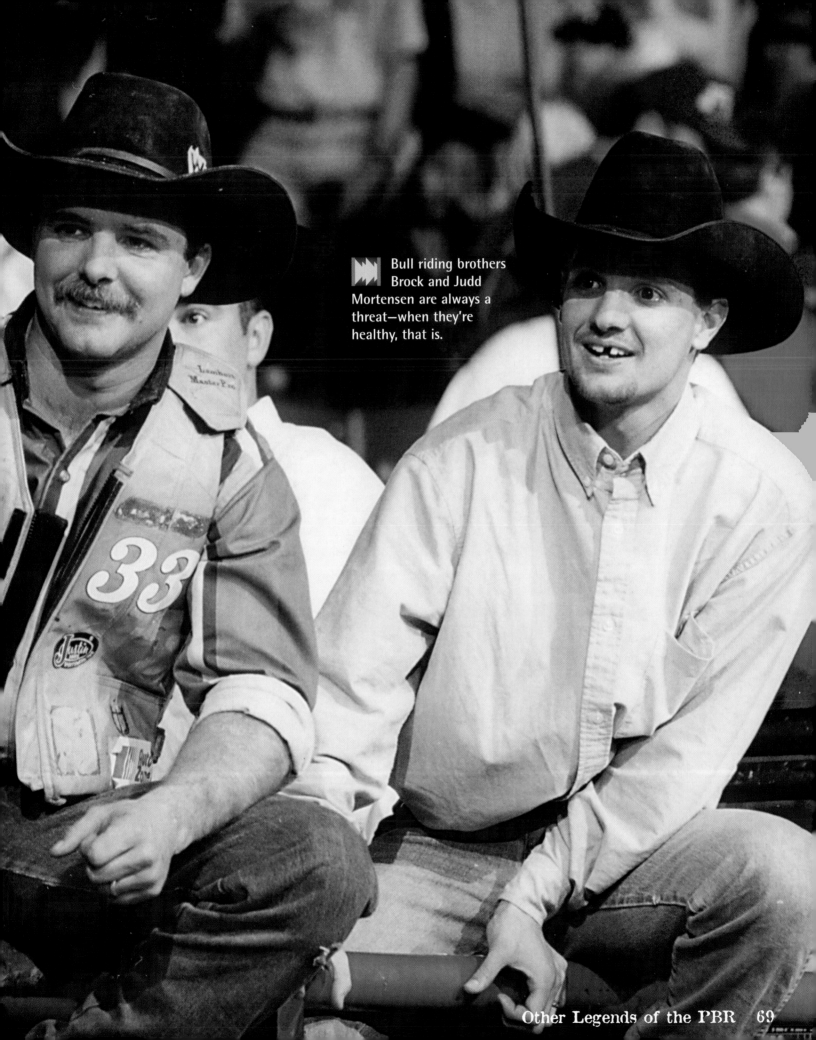

Bull riding brothers Brock and Judd Mortensen are always a threat—when they're healthy, that is.

Chris Shivers takes a flying leap at the St. Louis Open.

Bubba Dunn catches his breath after a sensational 96-point ride on Red Wolf in the opening round at the 1999 Jerome Davis Challenge in Charlotte.

Chris Shivers (above) was one of only three cowboys, including Ty Murray and Mike White, to make the whistle on all five bulls at the 1999 PBR Bud Light Cup World Championships.

Louisiana cowboy Bubba Dunn (left) co-owns the 96.5-point PBR record. Dunn turned in 96.5 big ones aboard Terry Williams' Promise Land at the Tampa, Florida, Bud Light Cup event in 1999, a mark Chris Shivers matched at the 2000 Tampa Open atop Williams and Logan's Jim Jam.

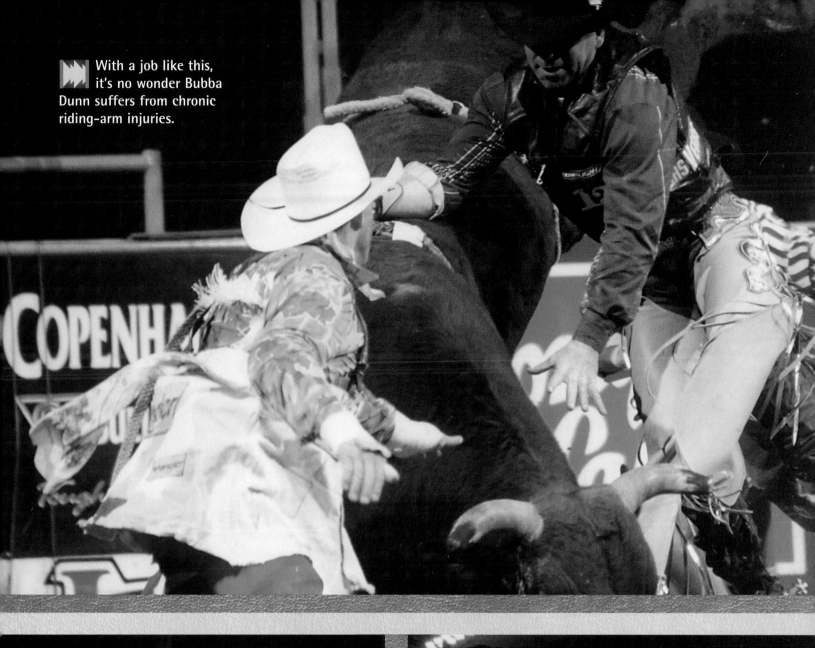

With a job like this, it's no wonder Bubba Dunn suffers from chronic riding-arm injuries.

Chris Shivers at work in his "office" at the 1999 PBR Finals. Shivers won the short round with 95 points on H.D. Page's Navajo.

Decked out in Mossy Oak camouflage, Bubba Dunn prepares to get down and dirty.

Friends and neighbors Ty Murray, Jim Sharp, and Tuff Hedeman harass each other behind the chutes. Sharp is one of only two men ever to have mastered Williams and Logan's dreaded Jim Jam. Sharp had a 94-point go-round with Jim Jam in the second round at the 1999 PBR Finals.

Seats are definitely optional when Chris Shivers rides. He's a 90-or-nothing kind of guy, and the fans love him for it.

Cody Lambert, Lane Frost, and Tuff Hedeman in a Panhandle Slim Western Wear advertisement. Hedeman's late, great best friend, 1987 PRCA World Champion Frost, died in the arena at the 1989 Cheyenne, Wyoming, Frontier Days Rodeo after taking a horn in the back. His life became the subject of the 1994 film *8 Seconds,* and he is remembered by bull riders and fans alike as one of the great stars of the sport.

Lane Frost's 1999 PBR Ring of Honor found a perfect fit on his dad Clyde's hand. If Lane Frost were still alive, he'd no doubt be a PBR wheelhorse.

Cody Lambert and announcer Bob Feist spoke of Lane Frost at PBR Finals 1999 as Frost's folks, Clyde and Elsie, accepted his PBR Ring of Honor. The Frosts were deeply touched by his friends' thoughtfulness ten years after their son's death.

Jim Shoulders, second from left, Cody Lambert, second from right, and announcer Bob Feist presented Donnie Gay, left, his PBR Ring of Honor at the 1997 PBR Finals.

Boys will be boys! Some things never change, and 1996 PBR Ring of Honor recipients Harry Tompkins and Jim Shoulders are living, breathing, riding proof of that. Here they are with Tompkins in the driver's seat and Shoulders bringing up the rear, riding a bull double for the pure fun of it at Madison Square Garden in New York in 1950.

Jim Shoulders is a sixteen-time PRCA world champion cowboy. He won more world titles in his career than any other cowboy in history.

Jim Shoulders lit up many a marquee in his rodeo heyday. He won his first world all-around title in 1949, and dominated the sport for years after that.

Larry Mahan
in his prime.

ProRodeo Hall of Famer Harry Tompkins was among the first recipients of the PBR Ring of Honor in 1996. Over a fourteen-year span Tompkins won two all-around championships, one bareback riding championship, and five bull riding championships. He was given the nickname of "Cat" because he almost always landed on his feet. His innovative chute design and better scoring and judging system are still being used today. Harry Tompkins ranks as one of the biggest stars in rodeo history.

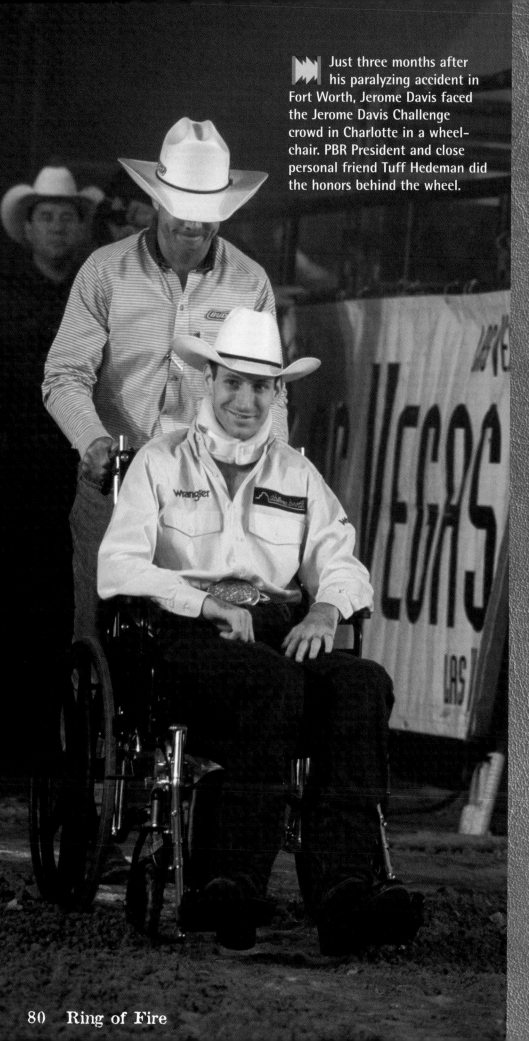

Just three months after his paralyzing accident in Fort Worth, Jerome Davis faced the Jerome Davis Challenge crowd in Charlotte in a wheelchair. PBR President and close personal friend Tuff Hedeman did the honors behind the wheel.

Cody Lambert and Tuff Hedeman were honored to present Larry "Bull" Mahan his PBR Ring of Honor at the 1998 PBR Finals. Lambert and Hedeman grew up idolizing Mahan, who over the years has been a hero to many.

Jerome Davis knocks out Bart Futrell's Hippie for 78 points at the Bud Light Cup event in Landover, Maryland. A ride like this one was practically a day off for Davis.

Cody Lambert, Tuff Hedeman, and announcer Bob Feist made the PBR Ring of Honor presentation to Jerome Davis at the 1998 Finals.

A broken neck couldn't stop Tuff Hedeman, shown here twisting one at the Billings, Montana, Bud Light Cup event in 1997. But that didn't surprise anyone who knew the story of how a young Tuff earned his nickname, saying nothing and not crying when his fingers were slammed in a truck door.

Cody Lambert and Tuff Hedeman grew up together in El Paso, Texas, so Lambert couldn't help but share a few of his favorite memories from the good old days when presenting his boyhood buddy his PBR Ring of Honor at the 1999 PBR Finals.

Cody Lambert, who learned a lot at Jerome Robinson's Bull Riding School when he was a kid, and announcer Bob Feist, right, look on as Robinson gets his first glance at his PBR Ring of Honor at the 1999 PBR Finals. In his role as PBR Production Manager, Robinson has been on the run with the PBR since day one.

A talent-packed pasture at the Terry Williams Ranch in Carthage, Texas. This shot, taken in 1997, includes five of the all-time greats (from left to right): 1996 PBR Bull of the Year Baby Face, 1999 PBR Bull of the Year and co-Bull of the Finals Promise Land, 1998 PBR Bull of the Year Moody Blues, 1997 PBR Bull of the Year Panhandle Slim, and the legendary Red Wolf, who some say is the greatest bucking bull of all time. Red Wolf has since been sold to the Herrington Cattle Company.

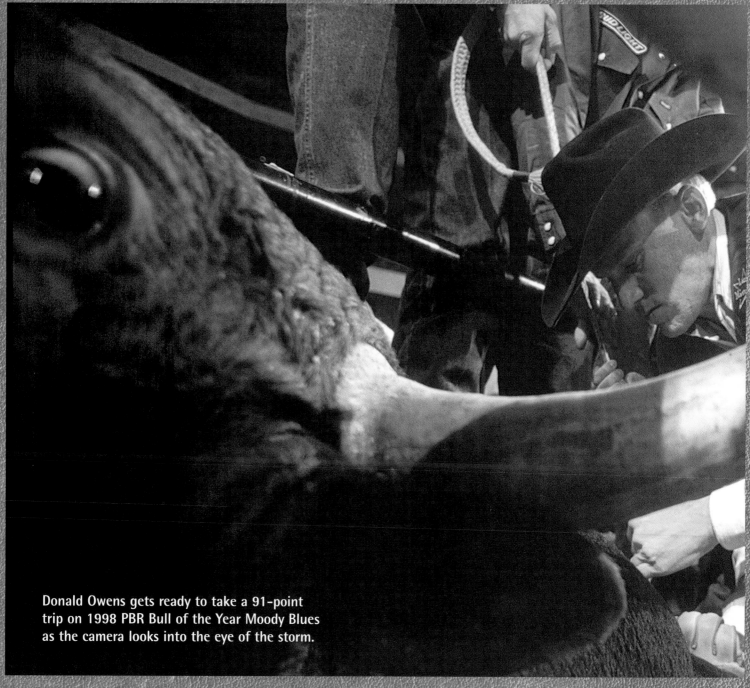

Donald Owens gets ready to take a 91-point trip on 1998 PBR Bull of the Year Moody Blues as the camera looks into the eye of the storm.

CHAPTER 4
THE FOUR-FOOTED LEGENDS OF THE PBR

Half of every cowboy's score is determined by the bull's performance; that is, how hard he is to ride. With that fundamental fact in mind, the PBR goes out of its way to seek out the greatest bucking bulls on earth and to reward their owners.

"When you have the supreme bull riders you better have the supreme bulls," said PBR Vice President and Livestock Director Cody Lambert. "You have to have one to appreciate the other. The term 'best' is used loosely by a lot of people. We don't go after the best bulls in town. We go after the best bulls in the world. The PBR is based on quality. And there's no way you can showcase the top cowboys on bulls high school kids could ride.

"The only way you can really prove that the forty-five guys on the PBR Bud Light Cup Tour are the best riders in the world is to pit them against worthy opponents. The bulls that buck in the PBR are becoming stars too, and they deserve it.

"All-star bull riders put out supreme efforts, whether they're riding indoors, outdoors, in one hundred–degree heat or freezing, drizzling rain. These bulls have that same quality. It doesn't matter if they're 1,500 miles from home, eating unfamiliar hay and grain they don't really like, may have stayed up a little too late last night or the ground's a little too soft—or whether they're in their own back yard, where they've bucked a hundred times before and know every inch of the terrain. They give it all they've got."

Like jockeys, bull riders tend to be on the smaller side. This is because there are inherent advantages in this sport to being compact. It's no coincidence that top 2000 contenders Chris Shivers and Ty Murray stand 5'3" and 5'8", respectively. But Owen Washburn, the 1996 PBR

Promise Land weighs two thousand pounds and, according to PBR Livestock Director Cody Lambert, is a lot more athletic than a bull his size ought to be. He jumps higher and spins faster than a bull of his build should be able to.

champ, is a strapping 6'2", and he's obviously learned to do a lot more than just get by. PBR bucking bulls come in all shapes and sizes too.

"You can tell some of these bulls are great athletes just by looking at them," Lambert said. "You can see by the way they carry themselves and walk around the pen that they can jump in the air and spin as fast as they want to. Others look like somebody's milk cow or a little stuffed teddy bear that belongs in a petting zoo somewhere."

Luckily for that type of bull, looks mean nothing in the PBR. It's performance that pays around here—and does it ever. The PBR and the Featherlite Trailers company join forces each year and put their money where their mouths are when it comes to the importance of stellar stock.

The $100,000 bull bonus program, which is paid in addition to fees paid each time a bull bucks throughout the season, doles out big money in three categories: PBR Bull of the Year, PBR Bull of the Finals, and PBR High-Money Bull.

"The PBR Bull of the Year is the most outstanding, hardest-to-ride bull out there," Lambert said. "He's the bull that tries as hard as he can to buck you off every time but without phony tricks, like trying to hit you in the face or scrape you off on the gate leaving the chute. He has no cheap shots to him, and when you ride him you're going to win it. The PBR Bull of the Year gets ridden seldom, if ever."

By a vote of the top forty-five bull riders in the world, Terry Williams' Promise Land took top honors in the PBR Bull of the Year category in 1999. "Promise Land is more athletic than a bull his size [two thousand pounds] should be," Lambert said. "He jumps higher and

because the first time I saw Promise Land he was a nice little spinner, too."

Other PBR Bulls of the Finals have included Don Kish's Copenhagen Cash in 1998, Dan Russell's Nitro in 1997, and James Harper's Strawberry Wine in 1996.

spins faster than you would think he could. He'll spin either direction, kicks high in the back end and drops in the front end, and any time he's ridden you'll see a score in the 90s."

Past PBR Bulls of the Year include Williams' Moody Blues in 1998, Williams' Panhandle Slim in 1997, Williams' Baby Face in 1996, and Sammy Andrews' Bodacious in 1995.

The PBR Bull of the Finals is chosen by a vote of the four judges at the World Championships, who in 1999 declared a tie between Promise Land and Jim Gay's Dillinger. At the 1999 Finals, Terry Don West racked up 96 points on Promise Land to share the second-round victory lap with Chris Shivers, who managed to match moves with Dan Russell's Trick or Treat Skoal. Aaron Semas attempted Promise Land in the short

round but got his clock cleaned. At Dillinger's first PBR Finals in 1999, he dumped both Bubba Dunn and Justin McBride.

"Dillinger is about a 1,900-pound, black, white-face bull with a brown line down his back," Lambert said. "The first time I saw Dillinger buck, which was a couple years ago, he looked like a good spinner that guys should love to draw. Two years later, he's developed into one of the rankest bulls in the world. This must be some kind of pattern,

James Harper and Claude Kimberlin's Gusto was named the 1999 PBR High-Money Bull based on cowboy go-round earnings won on his back before the PBR Finals. "Gusto is a 1,400-pound black bull with small horns that spins to the left as soon as they open the gate, with lots of speed," said Lambert. "Every time he gets ridden five or six seconds, he switches back to the right and spins just as fast. The guys love to draw him because they know if they ride him, they'll win. But if they take him too lightly they'll be surprised." Basically, the High-Money Bull is the one the cowboys want. He's no slam dunk, mind you—stub a toe and you're

Dillinger is a black, 1,900-pound bull with a white face and a brown line down his back.

dust. But strut your best stuff and you can keep on strutting all the way to the pay window.

"The money bull is the ultimate over-achiever," Lambert explained. "He's the bull with the biggest heart. He might not have the athletic ability and moves it takes to get Bud Light Cup guys on the ground every time, but he gives it all he's got and seldom gets ridden at the rodeos. The money bull is every bit as good a bull as the bull of the year, he's just not as great an athlete. The money bull gets ridden at the PBR Bud Light Cup events on a daily basis and averages a score in the high-80s every day. You might not win first in the round on him, but you'll always win a big check if you can ride him. The only way you get beat if you ride the money bull is if somebody else rides one of the PBR Bull of the Year candidates."

Past winners of the PBR High-Money Bull award include Williams' Promise Land in 1998, Jerome Robinson's Shotgun Red in 1997, Sammy Andrews' High Voltage in 1996, and Williams' Baby Face in 1995.

In addition to the $100,000 in bonus bucks for the owners of the buckingest bulls out there, Featherlite donates a twenty-four-foot aluminum gooseneck trailer to the man voted

MVP among the stock con-tractors. Terry Williams has been that man five years running, which is every year the award has been given.

"This is as good as it gets for me," Williams said. "To be the best, you've got to love this sport more than anything besides your fam-ily, and when it comes to the sport of bull riding, I do. That's what it's all about. You've got to love it to put everything into it, and if you don't put everything into it, it's not going to work. I love this sport and I love the people in it—that's my bottom line. It's like a big family to me. If I didn't feel that way, I'd do something else."

Williams does love the PBR's people, and the feeling is mutual all around. But his bulls are his babies, and he treats them like royalty. He hauls them at night, when the tempera-ture's cool. And on a really hot day he's been known to fill their water tanks with Gatorade to keep their electrolyte levels on the up and up. "They have to be in good shape to give it 100 percent," he said. "And, just like the rest

Moody Blues isn't exactly easy on the eyes, but beauty has nothing to do with bucking ability or points potential.

of us, they have to love their job to be good at it."

Like Lambert, Tuff Hedeman's no smoke-blower. He calls it like he sees it, straight down the line. "Terry's bulls are unbeliev-able," Hedeman said. "Nobody's put out more effort at this than Terry, and it shows. The stock contracting business is just as competitive as the riding today. If there's a good bull out there, it doesn't matter if he's in New Jersey, Florida, or Washington State—one of these guys will find out about him and go get him. We've always tried to make sure that PBR was good for the con-tractors, too, and have tried to keep their pay on the rise right along with the prize money, because the bulls are half the sport."

In the fall of 1999 Williams was on the receiving end of a record-breaking $200,000 bull deal in which he sold four of the sport's true headliners—Red Wolf, Hollywood, Moody Blues, and Locomotive Breath—to the Herrington Cattle Company.

"Over the long haul, we'll recoup that," said an unfazed Chad Herrington, whose partner in the deal is his dad, Robbie. "The PBR fan base will double, triple—who knows where it'll end. And the bulls are a big part of this sport."

Hollywood's a flashy, 90-or-nothing type of bull. He belonged to Terry Williams until being pur-chased in the bull deal of the century by the Herrington Cattle Company in 1999.

The Four-Footed Legends of the PBR 87

▶▶▶ Owen Washburn earned 95.5 points the hard way when he rode Promise Land to victory the night after Glen Keeley died trying to ride him in Albuquerque.

Moody Blues keeps cowboys honest. You can't set a trap for him and if you get too far ahead of him or behind him, you're toast. He's also built for speed. Here he is making Pete Hessman dizzy.

J.W. Hart, who's hanging on here with little more than heart and a few fingertips, knocked out 1997 PBR Bull of the Year Panhandle Slim for 94 points and the opening-round win at the 1998 PBR Finals.

Michael Gaffney takes his best shot at Baby Face.

The last ride of Tuff Hedeman's PBR championship season was aboard Sammy Andrews' Bodacious, 1995 PBR Bull of the Year, in the short round at that year's Finals. While the ride started out fine, it was about to take a terrifying turn for the worse. Follow the photos on the next two pages (starting clockwise from the bottom left of this page) as Bodacious gives Hedeman the ride of his life. (Photo 1) Hedeman handled Bodacious' first few jumps without a hitch, using perfect form. (Photos 2 through 4) Then, when Hedeman's body was moving forward, Bodacious threw back his head in what became a deadly Sunday-punch move. (Photo 5) The impact of this fall would have killed most mortals. Hedeman lay stunned and helpless on the arena floor.

(Top photo) An obviously shaken Cody Lambert scrambled to his old friend's side as bullfighters Joe Baumgartner and Loyd Ketchum moved in and formed a human shield between Bodacious and Hedeman.

(Bottom photo) The head-on collision between man and beast broke every bone in Hedeman's face. He would later undergo major facial reconstruction in an attempt to repair the damage.

Bullfighters and the Justin SportsMedicine Team, including Dr. Tandy Freeman (right), rushed to Hedeman's side. While everyone else was at the world championship awards banquet that night, Hedeman was at the hospital with his head swollen to the size of a basketball.

HEALTHSOUTH

DOUBLE-H *Boots*

Dillinger belonged to Jim Gay when he was named the co-Bull of the PBR Finals with Promise Land in 1999. He's since been sold to the Herrington Cattle Company. Slinging cowboys is Dillinger's favorite pastime. Here, Leslie Doyle gets a dose of Dillinger's bad medicine.

In the opinion of PBR Livestock Director Cody Lambert, who studies bulls on a daily basis and contracts them for the Bud Light Cup events, Red Wolf is the greatest bucking bull of all time.

Dan Russell's Nitro was the 1997 PBR Bull of the Finals. Here, bullfighter Frank Newsom distracts Nitro from a fallen bull rider in round-one action at the 1997 PBR Finals.

Don Kish's Copenhagen Cash, the 1998 PBR Bull of the Finals, is the son of legendary PRCA Bucking Bull of the Year Mr. T. Here, Terry Don West takes a ride on Cash.

Troy Dunn, left, and Featherlite Trailers' Paul Sween, right, listen to announcer Bob Feist deliver praises to perennial PBR Stock Contractor of the Year Terry Williams at the 1999 PBR Finals.

Chad Herrington and Terry Williams shake on their historic $200,000 bull deal at the 1999 PBR Finals. In the transaction, the Herrington Cattle Company took title to four of Williams' headliners.

Frank Newsom puts his own personal
twist on the Texas two-step in this save.

CHAPTER 5
THE PBR DANGER ZONE

There's an old saying in bull riding: "It's not *if* you'll get hurt riding bulls, but *when* and *how bad*." No matter how well you ride or how tough you are, if you play this game long enough your time on the stretcher will come. The danger factor is definitely there, and it's part of what attracts everyone involved with the sport, from the cowboys themselves to the spectators and sponsors.

There are some safety measures taken. Cody Lambert came up with a protective vest a few years back that's prevented countless life-threatening and fatal injuries. And PBR hires only the best cowboy lifesavers—they call them bullfighters—in the business, judged by a vote of the contestants whose very lives are on the line. It's a bullfighter's job to take bullets for the bull riders, to distract the bulls' attention and give cowboys a better chance at safe getaways.

"Bullfighters are so often faced with two choices—him or me," Ty Murray said. "The great ones don't hesitate to take the hit. The greatest bullfighters often go unnoticed because they undo wrecks before they happen. You can't put a value on what they're worth."

When bull riders get jerked down hard and thrown into harm's way, often under the hooves of a one-ton man-eater, they might as well have a bull's-eye tattooed across their foreheads. That's when the bullfighters really have to show what they're made of.

"There are times when it's a war," Cody Lambert said. "A bullfighter can stand back and watch or he can step in and be the opponent. The best bullfighters don't hesitate to think about it. They signed on to do a job and they do it. I think the same traits that make a bull rider great—being tough and determined—are what it takes to be a great bullfighter.

"All I really ask of a bullfighter is that if the bull rider gets hooked, he shares that hooking with him. There's a lot more to it than that, but the bottom line is it takes guts to fight bulls just like riding bulls does. Everyone who wears cleats and makeup is not a good bullfighter, and mediocre bullfighters are over-rated because you're basically on your own. On the other hand, the great ones are under-rated, because they make you feel like you'd go anywhere and get on any bull because there's no bull too mean when they're there."

Bullfighters take great pride in their cowboy-protecting careers and, like the riders, are on a constant quest for new-and-improved moves. "I love working PBR events because it's an honor to be able to fight bulls for the best bull riders in the world," said PBR bullfighting regular Joe Baumgartner. "It's also easier to help them, in a way, because they're pros. At the PBR level, when guys start to get in a wreck, they can start to get out of it on their own. They're that talented and that intelligent."

Jimmy Anderson often trolls the trenches with Baumgartner. At forty-seven, Anderson's a dinosaur in this young man's game. But there's nothing obsolete about him. He's still got the moves and he continues to crave contact. "The PBR is perfect for me because I can go to an event over a weekend and then rest up during the week," Anderson said. "I've had five knee surgeries, a shoulder rebuilt, and a plate and five screws in an ankle. But I love my job."

Tuff Hedeman's brother Gary, who also answers to "Roach," gets a rush out of great rescues. "I love it because it gives me the gratification of knowing that what I do can make a difference in somebody's life," Hedeman said. "Bull riders can continue to go down the road and make a living for their families because of what I do."

Just as undiscriminating bulls cut no deals with cowboys based on status, bullfighters are equal-opportunity lifesavers. "I will save every guy who nods his head, whether he's got a gold buckle or if he's a rookie from nowhere," said PBR bullfighting great Frank Newsom. "I think the guys are more appreciative than ever about what we do for them. It's our job to save lives."

Bullfighting is very serious business. But when a stubborn bull throws a kink in the production of a performance, the barrelman steps in to lighten the mood and close the gap in the action. Flint Rasmussen is one such comic, who dazzles crowds with his dance moves, too.

"Anyone can put on makeup, stand in a barrel, and tell jokes," Rasmussen said. "I very rarely tell jokes. I take real things that have happened and put a funny twist on them. I'm having the time of my life. I'm having a blast."

But there are times when the world's most dangerous sport proves itself worthy of that billing—when there's nothing anyone

Bullfighters Jimmy Anderson, Frank Newsom, Joe Baumgartner, and barrelman
Flint Rasmussen have all worked the PBR Finals the last few years.

can do to change the tragic outcome. Lane Frost, the charismatic 1987 PRCA champ of the world, lost his life in the arena at the 1989 Cheyenne Frontier Days Rodeo. Brent Thurman became the first Finals fatality when he died after being stepped on during the last performance of the 1994 National Finals Rodeo.

PBR suffered its first fatality in 2000 when Canadian champion Glen Keeley died from internal injuries in Albuquerque, New Mexico, after being stepped on by 1999 PBR Bull of the Year Promise Land. The best bullfighters in the world were there and did all they could. Keeley wore a protective vest. Nonetheless, the end result was as bad and sad as it gets.

"Glen knew just like all the rest of us know how dangerous this sport is, but he loved it and that's part of why he loved it," Tuff Hedeman said. "Every day these guys go to work there's always that risk. Glen started a great ride on a world champion bull. They were doing battle. About five seconds into the ride, Promise Land threw him off, just like he does most guys who get on him and, unfortunately, a guy who doesn't let go' til the bitter end is going to end up underneath more bulls than other guys. This was not an intentional act on Promise Land's part. He was just doing his job, like he always does. There was nothing the bullfighters, the doctors, or anyone else could have done that would have changed the outcome. The fact

is, this is just an extremely dangerous sport."

The Justin SportsMedicine Team is on hand at every PBR Bud Light Cup stop, and the faces of those like JST Director of Medical Services Dr. Tandy Freeman, Dr. J. Pat Evans, Dave Lammers, Rich Blyn, Mike Rich, Rick Foster, and Don Andrews are the first ones that injured cowboys see. The Justin SportsMedicine Program in association with HealthSouth provides invaluable medical services that range from first aid in the arena to surgical repairs and follow-up rehabilitation programs. HealthSouth is the nation's largest provider of comprehensive sports medicine, ambulatory surgery, and outpatient rehabilitation. The Justin SportsMedicine Program and HealthSouth are the official healthcare providers of the PBR.

The Justin Cowboy Crisis Fund has lent a long-standing financial hand up to injured rodeo contestants and their families. And now there's also the Resistol Relief Fund, which exclusively assists bull riders in need at every level of the game, from youth, high school, and intercollegiate contestants to PBR cowboys.

"The Resistol Relief Fund is such an important organization for anyone injured in the sport of bull riding," Tuff Hedeman said. "This fund can literally make all the difference in the world for someone who has been injured. Now that we have this fund, we will be seeing guys return to the arena who even just two or three years ago would not have had the means to return to the sport."

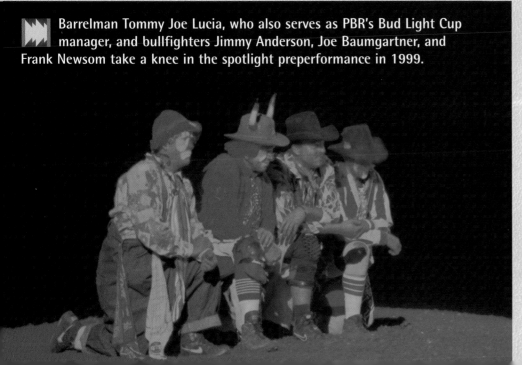

Barrelman Tommy Joe Lucia, who also serves as PBR's Bud Light Cup manager, and bullfighters Jimmy Anderson, Joe Baumgartner, and Frank Newsom take a knee in the spotlight preperformance in 1999.

Heads or tails? Joe Baumgartner takes the bow and leaves the stern to Jimmy Anderson in this save.

Roach Hedeman goes toe-to-toe with this bull. Roach, whose real name is Gary, is Red and Clarice Hedeman's sixth child. Tuff, their seventh, brought up the caboose in the Hedeman family.

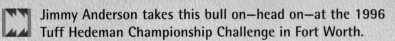 Jimmy Anderson closes the gap between this cowboy and the raging bull in hot pursuit.

Jimmy Anderson takes this bull on—head on—at the 1996 Tuff Hedeman Championship Challenge in Fort Worth.

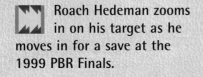 Roach Hedeman zooms in on his target as he moves in for a save at the 1999 PBR Finals.

Thanks, Frank! It's easy to understand why bullfighters are often referred to as "cowboy lifesavers," and why guys like Ty Murray say there isn't enough money in the world to pay them what they deserve.

Frank Newsom is one of the best bullfighters in the business because he's willing to take bullets for bull riders.

The best bullfighters in the world use teamwork to the cowboys' advantage. Here, Frank Newsom and Jimmy Anderson double-down on a dirty job.

Here's mud in your eye! Frank Newsom never sweats the small stuff. He never lets a little rain or mud slow him down, and this day in Tucson, Arizona, was no different.

That's no way to treat a champion. But then bulls can't read names on buckles, so they're equal-opportunity opponents. Owen Washburn understood that clause when he took the job.

116　Ring of Fire

Cowboys try to find their feet as fast as they can after hitting the dirt—for very obvious reasons.

Owen Washburn can't be seen in this frame because he's headed to safety. But when the dust settled, Washburn was the first to shake Frank Newsom's hand.

Frank Newsom gets knee deep into his work in this save.

Royd Doyal, who suffered a broken neck at the 1999 National Finals Rodeo, was bucked down into no man's land in this wreck earlier in the 1999 season.

Feet don't fail me now! It looks like a dance, but this bull doesn't exactly have a waltz in mind.

Every cowboy wears chaps for safety and flair and, since Cody Lambert came up with the protective vest concept a few years back, they now also wear the vests. However most only use the protective headgear when they draw a bull notorious for jerking guys down. The drawbacks of protective headgear include hindered vision and increased risk of neck injury due to more weight on the head in the case of whiplash-causing wrecks. Here, Clint Branger thanks the crowd for their enthusiasm.

Bullfighers Frank Newsom, left, and Joe Baumgartner, right, sacrifice themselves to save a fallen cowboy.

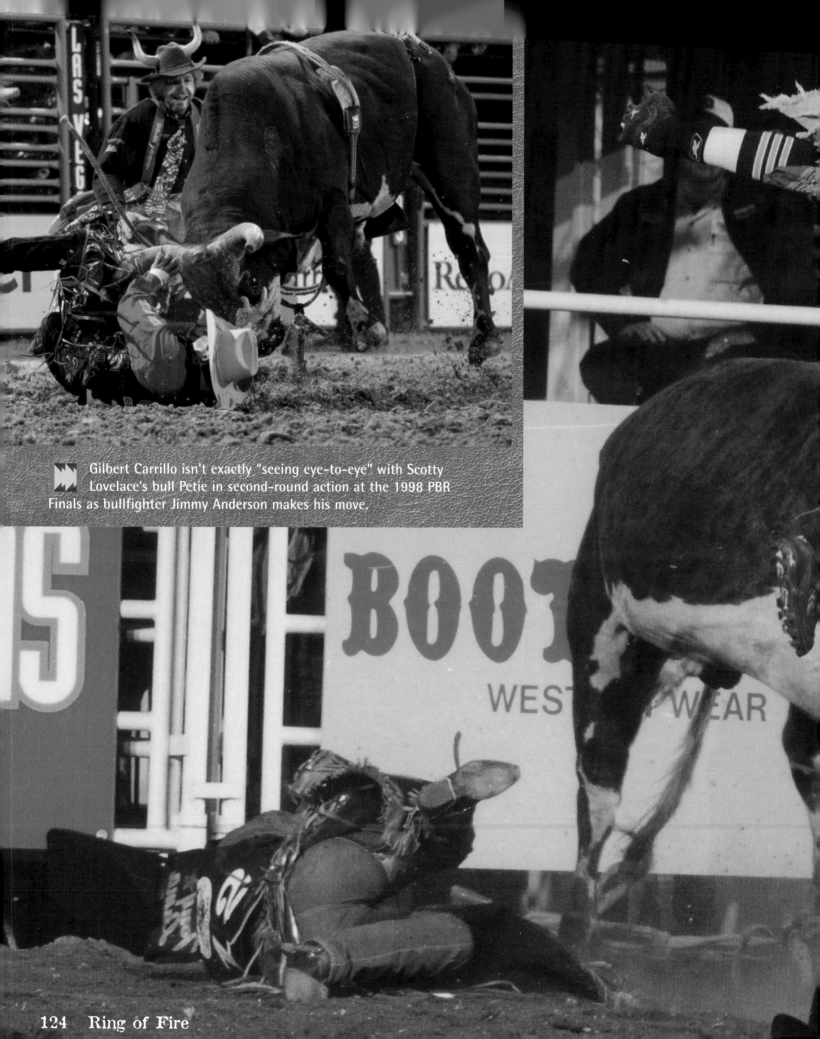

Gilbert Carrillo isn't exactly "seeing eye-to-eye" with Scotty Lovelace's bull Petie in second-round action at the 1998 PBR Finals as bullfighter Jimmy Anderson makes his move.

Getting a little air is all in a day's work for longtime bullfighting great Jimmy Anderson.

With his power and grace, Frank Newsom could have been a ballet star. Instead, the bull riding arena is his stage.

Bullfighter Loyd Ketchum jumps between Aaron Semas and imminent danger at the 1998 Bull Riding Blowout in Boise, Idaho.

Loyd Ketchum flags a bull down to distract him from a fallen cowboy.

Dennis Johnson gives this bull a love tap to get his attention while Roach Hedeman moves in from the other side.

 Loyd Ketchum uses his wheels so this cowboy can use his without the bull "horning in" on his business.

When a snot-snorting bull draws near, barrelman Flint Rasmussen gets down into his foxhole. By the time impact occurs, barrelmen are completely out of sight.

Barrelman Flint Rasmussen and bull rider Brock Mortensen yuck it up after everyone walks away from what could have been a gnarly episode.

Flint Rasmussen is flat funny, and nobody can fill a pause in the action caused by an uncooperative bull or a television delay like he can.

Ty Murray and Tuff Hedeman bow their heads for a solemn moment of silence in memory of Glen Keeley the night after he was killed at the 2000 Ty Murray Invitational in Albuquerque.

An unknown cowboy at the 1995 National Western Stock Show and Rodeo in Denver wearing a button in remembrance of Brent Thurman, the first cowboy ever killed at the National Finals Rodeo, in 1994.

Canadian Champion bull rider Glen Keeley knocks out Double J Rodeo Palace's Clayton's Pet for 93.3 points at the 2000 St. Louis Open in February. Keeley was killed the following month.

▞ Dr. Tandy Freeman, second from left, and a few of his friends and patients, cowboy superstars Jim Sharp, Ty Murray, and Tuff Hedeman. This shot was taken in 1997, not long after Freeman reconstructed Murray's riding-arm shoulder. Freeman has reconstructed both of Murray's shoulders and knees.

▞ The Justin SportsMedicine Team's Dr. Tandy Freeman fits Ty Murray with an arm brace at the 1999 PBR Bud Light Cup event in Oklahoma City. They both tried to make it work after Murray hyperextended his riding-arm elbow at a PRCA rodeo that summer but, being realists, they agreed it was best for Murray to sit out both Oklahoma City and Houston on his road to recovery.

▞▞ The Justin SportsMedicine crew, led by Dr. Tandy Freeman, carried Troy Dunn out of the 1998 PBR Finals arena after he dislocated his left hip in first-round action. Dunn watched the rest of the Finals from the sidelines, but his regular-season points carried him to the PBR crown.

Cody Lambert and Tandy Freeman were on hand for Tuff Hedeman's induction into the ProRodeo Hall of Fame in Colorado Springs in August 1997. Lambert is one of Hedeman's oldest, closest friends, and Hedeman has referred to Freeman as the "MVP of the PBR."

A grateful Ty Murray lays a wet one on Dr. J. Pat Evans, one of the founding fathers of the Justin SportsMedicine Program and an old friend to the cowboys, at the 2000 Tuff Hedeman Championship Challenge in Fort Worth.

Dave Lammers, with his Wrangler pockets to the camera, Tandy Freeman, and other members of the Justin SportsMedicine crew attend to a fallen soldier in the battlefield.

Dan Russell's Shorty ran the length of Chris Shivers several times in this nightmarish mauling at the 1998 Bull Riding Blowout in Boise, Idaho. Eyewitnesses, including Shivers' traveling partner Norman Curry, who bailed off the back of the chutes in the rescue attempt, say it's a miracle Shivers survived. With a little help from an unstoppable spirit, a Cody Lambert Master Pro protective vest, a stretcher, and an oxygen tank, Shivers let his fans know he'd be back to do battle another day.

Luke Perry as the late, great Lane Frost.

CHAPTER 6
FAME AND FORTUNE

8 SECONDS

In 1994, five years after his untimely death in the arena, Hollywood paid tribute to the life of Lane Frost with a silver-screen salute they called *8 Seconds*. Luke Perry starred as Frost, Stephen Baldwin played Tuff Hedeman, Red Mitchell portrayed Cody Lambert, and Cynthia Geary played Frost's widow, Kellie.

Perry, perhaps best known for his part as Dylan Mackay on the popular television series *Beverly Hills, 90210*, knew from the start that he'd have to roll up his sleeves and get dirty in order to get to know Lane's real-life friends and character.

"You don't just walk into a room of Jim Sharps, Ty Murrays, Clint Brangers, Cody Lamberts, and Tuffs [Hedeman] and say, 'Yeah, I'm going to be a bull rider. And I'm going to start tomorrow,'" said Perry, who bears a striking resemblance to Frost. "These guys know. They were there. They lived it. A lot of times [during filming] I'd be pulling my rope and Cody would stop me and say, 'Hold it. Lane wouldn't do it like that.'"

Perry was no stranger to the spotlight when he got involved in the project. But he had no clue about Frost or bull riding. So he did something about it.

"To get my head and heart in the right place, spending time with the cowboys was the best way to do it," he said. "The bull riders were lined up, ready to help, with smiles on their faces. Lane left behind him a tremendous legacy of love and integrity. He gave a lot of people someone to look up to. Here was a guy whose life story was worth telling."

This Gold Record Award, which includes music from the film *8 Seconds*, was presented to Clyde and Elsie Frost, parents of the late cowboy hero Lane Frost, by Reba McEntire.

In an effort to truly understand their characters, Perry and Baldwin even went so far as to try their hands in a bull rope. "I don't know any other actor who could say, 'Baldwin, let's go ride some bulls, buddy,'" Baldwin said of Perry. "I said, 'I'm there.' Hey, I'm from Long Island; he's from Ohio." But that didn't stop them from throwing themselves headfirst into the culture of bull riding.

After getting the part, Baldwin first met Hedeman at La Fiesta de los Vaqueros, the PRCA rodeo in Tucson, Arizona. He'll never forget the first chance he had to get to know his character in person. "I asked Tuff why I was the only guy there with pointy boots," Baldwin remembers. "He said, 'I guess you're just the only guy out here who wants to look stupid.' When he said that, I wanted to play him. Cowboys have the humblest sense of fearlessness I've ever seen. They're honest, respectful, real, true, and genuine."

Perry was equally impressed with what he found behind the bucking chutes. "These people are athletes," he said. "Cowboys devote their lives to becoming the best. It requires more sacrifice than most sports, and these guys do it for the love of the sport. That's the best reason. This movie shows the world—through the eyes of this champion—what this sport's about."

Frost was the magnet that drew director John Avildsen, the Academy Award–winning director of *Rocky* and *The Karate Kid*, to the script. "I knew zip about rodeo before I got involved in this movie," Avildsen said. "But I'd never seen a boxing match before I did *Rocky*. The kind of man he [Frost] was is what attracted me to this project."

As the promotional poster for *8 Seconds* read, "The sport made him a Legend. His heart made him a Hero."

RING OF FIRE

The sport of professional bull riding is returning to the silver screen in a big way in 2001 with the release of *Ring of Fire*, which includes scenes filmed at the 1998 PBR Bud Light Cup World Championships.

Written by James Redford and directed by Academy Award winner Xavier Koller, *Ring of Fire* stars Marcus Thomas as professional bull rider Ely Braxton and Kiefer Sutherland as his bull-fighting brother Hank. Hank and Ely are the sons of champion bull rider Reid Braxton, who's played by Pete Postelthwaite. Ely's been strongly encouraged to hang up his chaps after suffering life-threatening injuries at the hooves of a bull. But he won't be satisfied until he takes his best shot at the title.

In his search to see if he's still got the right stuff, not to mention whatever it takes to earn the approval of his long-estranged father, Ely gets involved with Hank's long-time obsession, barrel racer Celia Jones, who's played by Daryl Hannah. As the season-long road winds its way toward the finals, this brotherly bond gets tested right along with Ely's bull-riding skills. True to the sport, in the end it all rides on eight seconds.

"There are only two ways you can ride a bull," Sutherland says. "You can either make it happen or you can let it happen."

Luke Perry, star of *8 Seconds*, with director John Avildsen, on the film's set near San Antonio.

Tracy and Tuff Hedeman, Luke Perry, and Cody and Leanne Lambert at the 1994 world premiere party for *8 Seconds*. Said Perry, "To get my head and heart in the right place, spending time with the cowboys was the best way to do it. The bull riders were lined up, ready to help, with smiles on their faces."

Ring of Fire's other stars include Molly Ringwald, who plays Ely's girlfriend Connie, and Melinda Dillon, who portrays Ely and Hank's mom, Rose. A number of real-deal PBR cowboys, including Terry Don West, Chris Shivers, David Fournier, Curt Lyons, and Adriano Moraes, are recognizable in the film, as are bullfighters Joe Baumgartner and Roach Hedeman.

Screenwriter James Redford, who's the son of Robert Redford, grew up in New York City. But he spent most of his childhood summers and vacations in Sundance, Utah, which "guaranteed that I'd seen a lot of rodeos." What really impressed the young Redford was "the range of emotions . . . the events and the people involved displayed a combination that encompassed terror and humor all at the same time."

Redford spent the late 1980s and early 1990s living in Colorado, where his fascination with the sport continued to grow. "I spent a great deal of time at the National Western Stock Show and Rodeo [in Denver], where a character began to take shape in my mind," Redford recalled.

Witnessing Lane Frost's death in the arena at the 1989 Cheyenne Frontier Days Rodeo had a profound effect on Redford, who completed the first draft of this script in 1990. "That incident inspired a multitude of ideas for the character I had been formulating," Redford

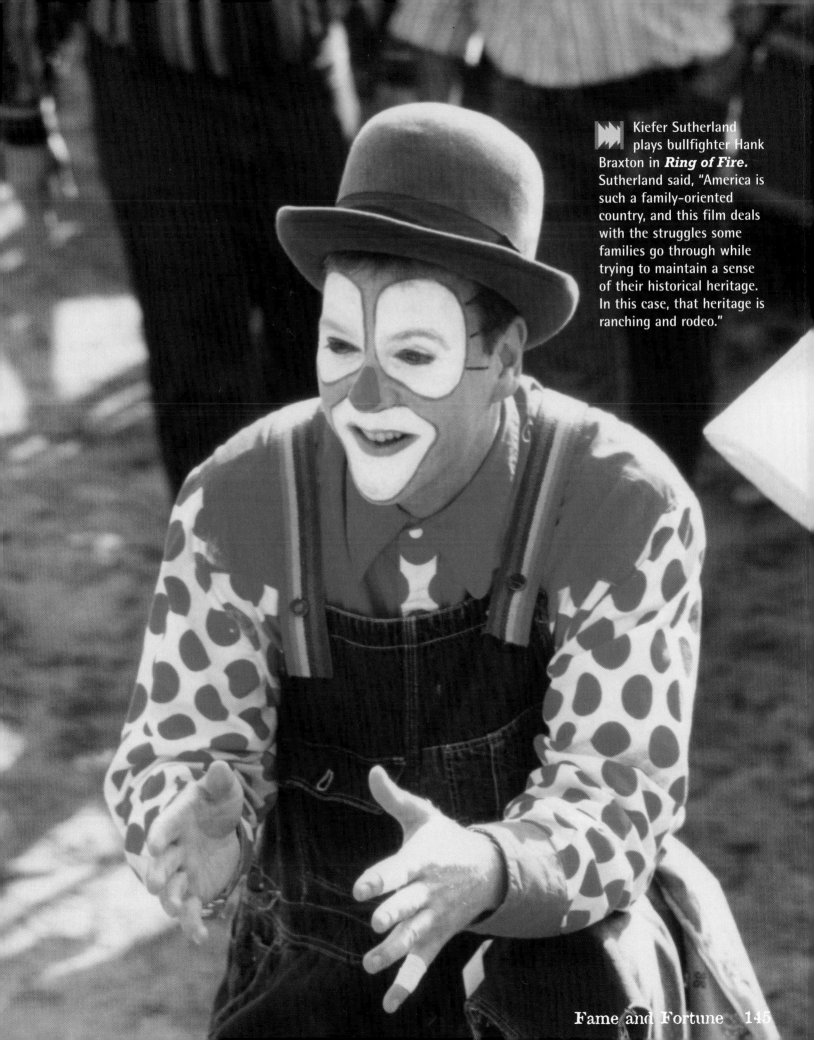

Kiefer Sutherland plays bullfighter Hank Braxton in *Ring of Fire.* Sutherland said, "America is such a family-oriented country, and this film deals with the struggles some families go through while trying to maintain a sense of their historical heritage. In this case, that heritage is ranching and rodeo."

continued. "After Lane's death, I began to think about the incident in terms of the family—how my character's struggle with his own identity not only affected him but also the consequences his family would endure because of his turmoil."

Sutherland, a longtime competitive team roper in real life, jumped at the chance to play Hank. "The most important reason I wanted to do this part was the script," said Sutherland, who's gained notoriety and popularity over the years with memorable roles in such films as *Flatliners* and *A Few Good Men*. "America is such a family-oriented country, and this film deals with the struggles some families go through while trying to maintain a sense of their historical heritage. In this case, that heritage is ranching and rodeo."

Actor Marcus Thomas made his debut performance with a starring role in *Ring of Fire*. "We were looking for a young actor who didn't bring any kind of myth of stardom attached to him," explained Koller, who earned his Academy Award for *Journey of Hope* in 1990. "We wanted a fresh face in the role and, even though we took a risk with Marcus, he grew very fast and delivered everything we had hoped he would."

Thomas spent time both in the arena and on a ranch while getting into Ely's character. "There is this incredible culture in the middle of America that I knew nothing about," Thomas said. "Despite the fact that the benefits, both monetarily and from a health point of view, are tenuous at best, there is a unique magnetism that draws these people to this sport. After living the life for a few weeks, I understood where some of that comes from."

One of the greatest challenges in filming *Ring of Fire* was coming up with realistic footage of the actors riding bulls. A few carefully choreographed scenes show the actors at work in the arena. The rest were left to the real McCoy professionals. For example, PBR World Champion Owen Washburn stepped in as Thomas' stunt double.

"We did some very safe, limited aspects of it," Sutherland said. "But this is not a joke—something you can say, 'Oh, let me have a go at it.' It can kill you. You have to know what you're doing, and we've had some amazingly talented athletes come in and do that for us."

Like the script says, "This isn't sport—this is war."

Actress Daryl Hannah needed no stunt double to play barrel racer Cecilia Jones in *Ring of Fire*.

The filmmakers sought out the best of bull riding's best for the job, and found them in the cream of the PBR cowboy crop.

"Whenever the PBR can go Hollywood and be recognized as the governing body of bull riding, just as any film based on Major League Baseball or the NFL is, it will help bring awareness to our sport," said PBR CEO Randy Bernard. "That, in turn, will create new fans."

CHAMPIONSHIP BULL RIDING ON TNN

Television coverage has had a huge hand in the electrifying evolution of this sport. The PBR has captured the imaginations—and lit up the living rooms—of millions since it first hit TNN airwaves in 1994. The PBR craze seems to catch a gear at every turn and appears to be headed full steam ahead on a collision course with unfathomable new heights. That's a fact, and it has everything to do with TV.

"A lot of things have contributed to our success, but take away television and we might not be in business," Tuff Hedeman said. "If you don't have TV, you don't attract major sponsors. And without sponsors, you can't possibly be a big-money sport. That's why we're riding at the kind of money we are today. All truly successful sports are on television. With TV, you're able to expose a sport to millions of people who'd probably never go to the trouble of finding an event, buying a ticket, and attending. It never ceases to amaze me how many people now follow our sport who you'd never expect to be bull riding fans. City people, country people, and all kinds of mainstream people are now bull riding fans."

Hosted by Donnie Gay, Dan Miller, and Pam Minick, PBR's prime-time *Championship Bull Riding* program is TNN's highest-rated show. The TNN telecasts now reach more than 80 million homes.

"The only thing I dislike about the PBR Tour is that I'm in my forties instead of in my twenties," chuckled Gay, an eight-time PRCA world champion bull rider who calls it like he sees it on the telecasts. "This Tour is a cut above all others. I feel sorry for the people running the concession stands at these events. The only time these fans are going to buy anything is when they're walking in and walking out. People don't wander off for a hot dog when these guys are riding these bulls. And when you show this caliber of bull riding, it doesn't matter if you're a housewife or a ten-year-old kid or a seventy-year-old retiree. When you turn on this show, you're glued to the set."

▰ The TNN television crew, along with Dan Miller, Jerome Robinson, and Donnie Gay, discuss the best way to set up a shot.

▰ Several scenes for the film *Ring of Fire* were filmed at the 1998 PBR Bud Light Cup World Championships at the MGM Grand Garden Arena in Las Vegas. Here, it's the Justin SportsMedicine crew to the rescue.

Pam Minick inter-
views Aaron
Semas for the popular
***Championship Bull
Riding*** telecast on TNN.

Pam Minick quizzes Chris Shivers for a 2000 PBR telecast on TNN.

TNN cameraman Mark Voyles
zooms in on the arena action
at the St. Louis Open.

The sirens blare on every 90-point ride in the Bud Light Bull Pen, which is filled with bull riding enthusiasts at select Bud Light Cup stops.

 Donnie Gay, Tuff Hedeman, and Dan Miller call it like they see it on the TNN telecasts. Here they are seen at the 1999 PBR Bud Light Cup World Championships.

 J.W. Hart ponders a reporter's question.

Tuff Hedeman's little boy Trevor helps him with autographs during the 1999 PBR Finals. No one's autograph lines are longer than Hedeman's.

Bull riding and rodeo fans will never forget the legendary Lane Frost, who died in the arena at age twenty-five in 1989. Frost will live on forever in the hearts and minds of everyone ever exposed to his contagious smile. Here we see Frost fans with an autographed poster of the fallen hero.

PBR fans are some of the most enthusiastic in the sporting universe and their demographics are diverse. They're people of all ages who come from all walks of life. No one sits on his or her hands at a PBR event.

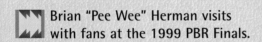 Brian "Pee Wee" Herman visits with fans at the 1999 PBR Finals.

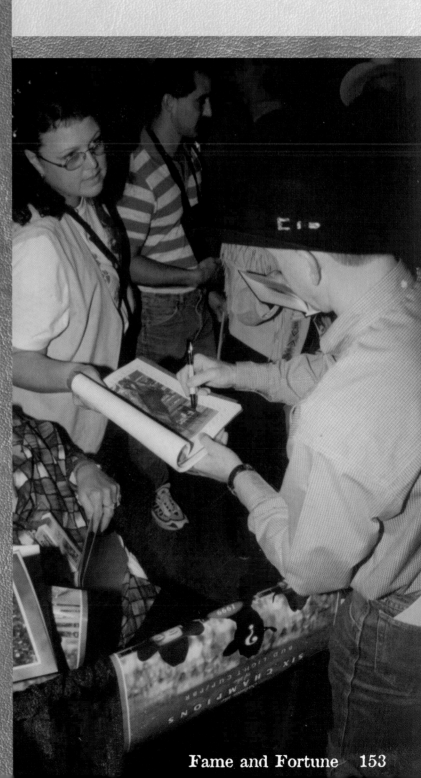

Charles Litchfield signs his John Hancock for a fan at the 1999 PBR Finals. PBR cowboys spend more time getting to know their fans than do athletes in most professional sports.

Ladies and gentlemen, Mr. Tuff Hedeman. Bull riding favorite Hedeman greets a rowdy crowd at the Jerome Davis Challenge in Charlotte, North Carolina.